Media Theory for A Level

Media Theory for A Level provides a comprehensive introduction to the 19 academic theories required for A Level Media study. From Roland Barthes to Clay Shirky, from structuralism to civilisationism, this revision book explains the core academic concepts students need to master to succeed in their exams. Each chapter includes:

- Comprehensive explanations of the academic ideas and theories specified for GCE Media study.
- Practical tasks designed to help students apply theoretical concepts to unseen texts and close study products/set texts.
- Exemplar applications of theories to set texts and close study products for all media specifications (AQA, Eduqas, OCR and WJEC).
- Challenge activities designed to help students secure premium grades.
- Glossaries to explain specialist academic terminology.
- Revision summaries and exam preparation activities for all named theorists.
- Essential knowledge reference tables.

Media Theory for A Level is also accompanied by the essentialmediatheory.com website that contains a wide range of supporting resources. Accompanying online material includes:

- Revision flashcards and worksheets.
- A comprehensive bank of exemplar applications that apply academic theory to current set texts and close study products for all media specifications.
- Classroom ready worksheets that teachers can use alongside the book to help students master essential media theory.
- Help sheets that focus on the application of academic theory to unseen text components of A Level exams.

Mark Dixon is an Eduqas A Level examiner and Head of Media and Film at Durham Sixth Form Centre. He is also a freelance author, and has written for *The Guardian*, *Tes*, *Media Magazine* and *Teach Secondary* as well as authoring a range of digital resources for Eduqas Media.

Media Theory for A Level
The Essential Revision Guide

Mark Dixon

Routledge
Taylor & Francis Group

LONDON AND NEW YORK

First published 2020
by Routledge
2 Park Square, Milton Park, Abingdon, Oxon OX14 4RN

and by Routledge
52 Vanderbilt Avenue, New York, NY 10017

Routledge is an imprint of the Taylor & Francis Group, an informa business

© 2020 Mark Dixon

British Library Cataloguing-in-Publication Data
A catalogue record for this book is available from the British Library

Library of Congress Cataloging-in-Publication Data
A catalog record has been requested for this book

ISBN: 978-0-367-14542-2 (hbk)
ISBN: 978-0-367-14543-9 (pbk)
ISBN: 978-0-429-03224-0 (ebk)

Typeset in Bembo
by Wearset Ltd, Boldon, Tyne and Wear

Visit the companion website: www.essentialmediatheory.com/

For Steph, Maisie and Preston

Contents

Media representation

Media industries

1   Semiotics

Roland Barthes

Until the 1950s academic study of culture was largely limited to an exploration of high culture. Literature, art, architecture, music, etc. were deemed worthy of study because, supposedly, they articulated sophisticated and nuanced modes of thinking. Popular culture, conversely, was rejected as unworthy of analysis because the stories told by advertising, cinema and the then emerging form of television were thought to be constructed with so little precision, and their effects so simple, that any academic attention was undeserving.

Barthes, however, realised that the mass media ought to be taken seriously, and his 1957 essay collection, *Mythologies*, stands as one of the first attempts to evaluate the finesse and impact of mass media narratives. Indeed, Barthes *Mythologies* revels in popular culture, analysing anything and everything from wrestling to horoscopes, from car adverts to political news. Barthes's writing intuited that mass media forms affected a deep presence within society – an ideological presence whose scope and influence far outstripped the nuanced reach of high culture.

Concept 1: denotation and connotation

Denotation/connotation

Barthes tells us that media products are decoded by their readers – in the first instance, at least – using what he calls a 'denotative reading'. Denotative readings, he suggests, occur when readers recognise the literal or physical content of media imagery. For example, a denotative reading of the 'I, Daniel Blake' poster in Figure 1.1 would simply acknowledge that the photograph depicts an older man who wears dark clothing with his fist raised in the air.

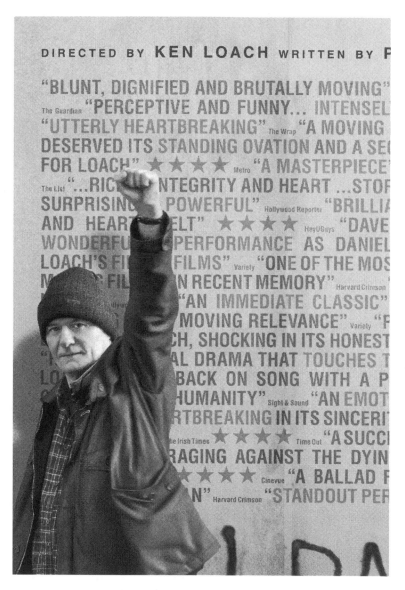

Figure 1.1 'I, Daniel Blake' film poster (2016).
© Sixteen Films.

Barthes tells us that readers quickly move beyond the simple recognition of image content and subsequently engage in what he calls 'connotative decoding'. Connotation, Barthes argues, 'makes possible a (limited) dissemination of meanings, spread like gold dust on the surface of the text' (Barthes, 2007, 9). Connotative readings, he suggests, refer to the deeper understandings prompted by media imagery and to the emotional, symbolic or even ideological significances produced as a result of those readings.

The 'I, Daniel Blake' poster in Figure 1.1, for example, signifies various meanings through a range of subtle cues: the raised fist suggests

Table 1.1 Connotative effects of photographic imagery

Image makers use a range of strategies to infer meaning within imagery – look out for the following when analysing the meaning making effects of your set texts.

Image features	Look out for
Pose Subject positioning, stance or body language	**Fourth wall breaks:** where the photographic subject meets the gaze of the audience. This can create a confrontational, aggressive or invitational feel. **Off-screen gaze:** upward gazes can suggest spirituality; right-frame gazes can suggest adventure or optimism; left-frame gazes can suggest regret or nostalgia. **Body language control:** might be open or closed, passive or active, strong or weak. **Subject positioning:** the way that group shots are arranged is usually significant with power conferred on those characters that occupy dominant positions. **Proxemics:** refers to the distance between subjects – the closer the characters are the closer their relationship. **Left-to-right/right-to-left movement:** characters who travel from screen left to screen right create positive connotations – they are adventurers and we might feel hopeful about their prospects; right-to-left movements can suggest failure or an impending confrontation.

continued

Image features	Look out for
Mise en scène Props, costume and setting	**Symbolic props:** props are rarely accidental – their use and placement generally infer symbolic meanings.
	Pathetic fallacy: settings and scenery often serve further symbolic functions – weather, for example, infers the tone of characters' thoughts.
	Costume symbolism: character stereotypes are constructed through costuming, helping us to decipher a character's narrative function.
Lighting connotations	**High-key lighting:** removes shadows from a scene, often producing a much lighter, more upbeat feel.
	Low-key lighting: emphasises shadows and constructs a much more serious set of connotations.
	Chiaroscuro lighting: high contrast lighting usually created through the use of light beams penetrating pitch darkness and connotes hopelessness or mystery.
	Ambient lighting: infers realism.
Compositional effects Shot distance, positioning of subjects within the frame	**Long shots:** imply that a subject is dominated by their environment.
	Close ups: intensify character emotion or suggest impending drama.
	Left/right compositions: traditionally the left side of the screen is reserved for characters with whom the audience is meant to empathise and vice versa.
	Open/closed frames: open framing suggests freedom, while enclosing a character within a closed frame can suggest entrapment.
	Tilt and eye line: tilt-ups and high eyelines convey power, while tilt-downs and low eyelines connote powerlessness and vulnerability.
Post-production effects	**Colour control:** colours are often exaggerated for specific connotative effect – red: anger; white: innocence; blue: sadness and so on.
	High saturation: colour levels are increased creating a cheerier, upbeat feel.
	Desaturation: taking colour out of an image generates a serious or sombre tone.

defiance, the character's costume infers poverty or that he comes from a working class background, while the dark clothing potentially constructs a sombre tone and suggests that the advertised film will deal with serious or tragic themes. In reading the meaning of these subtle cues, and of the multitude of clues that all media products present, audiences use their cultural knowledge and their experience of similar imagery to help them construct an understanding of a product's significance.

Text and image

Barthes, of course, understood that photographic imagery does not construct meaning by itself. Imagery, in print-based products, works alongside text-based components. Headers and taglines give meaning to photos, while photos themselves provide an accompanying visual explanation for news copy. The interplay between text and image, Barthes tells us, is determined by the positioning of textual components and by the relative size of each element. Barthes also details the use of text to 'anchor' image meanings in advertisements and print news. Photo captions, headers and taglines, Barthes tells us, guide readers towards defined significations.

Within the 'Tide' advertisement depicted in Figure 1.2, for instance, readers are encouraged to question why the woman is holding the box of washing powder in what looks, to all intents and purposes, to be a romantic embrace. The image presented could connote a whole range of meanings, from the surreal to the nonsensical. Has the woman actually fallen in love with a box of washing powder? Has she found real love as a result of the product? Perhaps, we might conclude, the woman has a strange washing powder fetish.

It is not until we read the strapline at the bottom of the advert, 'Tide gets clothes cleaner than any other washday product', that the meaning of the image is explicated. The woman loves Tide as a result of its cleaning powers. In the sense, the text component anchors the meaning of imagery. Without anchorage, Barthes suggests, media imagery is likely to produce polysemic connotations or multiple meanings. Anchorage, Barthes tells us, constructs, 'a vice which holds the connoted meanings from proliferating' (Barthes, 2007, 39).

Figure 1.2 Tide washing powder advert (1950).

Source: image courtesy of Advertising Archive.

Box 1.1 Apply it: diagnose the connotations constructed by media set texts

Use the following questions to help you construct a detailed analysis of the media language effects of relevant set texts:

Pose connotations

- Who is pictured within key imagery? And with whom? What kind of relationship do the characters have with each other?
- What is significant about their pose? Where is the character looking and in what ways is that significant?
- What does their body language reveal?

Mise en scène

- What is the significance or props, setting and costuming?
- Do costumes tell us who the character is or what role they play in the overarching narrative?

Lighting

- What kind of lighting is used and with what emotional or connotative effect?
- Who is placed in shadow? Who is given light?

Composition

- What sort of shot distance is used to depict the subject?
- Is the shot composed with the subject on the left or right side of the frame? What connotations does this positioning create for the audience?
- Is the shot constructed as an open or closed frame shot?
- Is tilt applied to the composition and with what effect?

Post-production

- What colours are foregrounded and with what connotative effect?
- Is colour taken out of the shot?

Anchorage

- What elements, if any, anchor the meanings constructed by your set texts?

Further set text help is available for a range of products for all exam boards at www.essentialmediatheory.com

Barthes five code symphony

Barthes's denotation/connotation model provides an excellent framework for analysing print media. We can use it to diagnose the effects of costume choices or settings, or to think about the significations created through shot distance or shot composition. Barthes's denotation/connotation model, however, is less effective when we have to consider the way in which elements combine to produce singular effects. Narratives, for instance, set up meanings at the start of stories that are connected to later narrative events – stories, for example, tease audiences with mysteries that are only resolved at the end. Similarly, some connotations are used throughout a text in a way that gives them a deeper connotative meaning than if they appeared just once. For example, the repeated use of food-oriented references in the Hansel and Gretel fairy tale – breadcrumbs, the gingerbread house, the cooking of the witch – creates an enhanced symbolic effect.

To account for this, Barthes produced a more nuanced version of his denotation/connotation model in which a symphony of five explicit coding effects are used to create meaning. These connotative effects, he argues, operate like voices or instruments in a band – sometimes playing in unison, while at other moments they are muted so that single codes can deliver solo effects.

Barthes details his five code symphony as follows:

- **Hermeneutic codes (enigmas):** construct moments of mystery to intrigue the reader or viewer. Enigmas also hook readers, compelling further reading or viewing to locate answers to the questions posed. The header of the 'Tide' advert in Figure 1.2, for instance, constructs a hermeneutic response through the header element. Readers are prompted to ponder what it is that 'women want', while the enigma is only resolved if the rest of the advert is consumed. Some products, Barthes tells us, rely on hermeneutic codes more than others – crime dramas, for instance, usually convey and reinforce long standing enigmas throughout their narratives.
- **Proairetic codes (actions):** narratives also offer moments in which meaning is conveyed through action or demonstration. Action provides explanation or excitement, sometimes working to resolve the enigmas that earlier narrative sequences might pose.

The depiction of the washing machine in the top right hand corner of the 'Tide' advert (Figure 1.2), for example, constructs a proairetic moment in that the imagery illustrates how the washing powder is used. Again, some products deploy proairetic codes more than others: science fiction, thrillers and crime dramas, for instance, typically rely on moments of concentrated action to generate viewer excitement.

- **Semantic codes (connotative elements):** refers to any element within a media text that produces a single connotative effect. Semantic codes include lighting, *mise en scène* and colour usage. They also refer to the use of compositional effects, pose or even to typographic decisions and the significations that text size or font selection convey. Semantic code connotations, for example, are created in the 'Tide' advert (Figure 1.2) via the wavelike arrangement of the 'What Women Want' header (connoting an upbeat jaunty tone), while the repeated use of exclamation marks throughout the advert construct energy and volume.

- **Symbolic codes:** semantic and symbolic codes are highly similar and often quite hard to tease apart. Perhaps one of the easiest ways to seek out the symbolic codes within a product is to search for repeated symbols that convey a deeper meaning. In television, symbolic codes often surface as repeated themes or visual motifs and are referenced throughout the story in a thread of continuous underlying meaning. In the 'Tide' advert (Figure 1.2), the repetition of the word 'clean' and the way that cleanliness in general is presented could be considered to be symbolic meaning making.

- **Cultural codes (referential codes):** refers to the inclusion of material that generates meaning from outside the product. Cultural codes might include the use of proverbs, sayings or idioms. They might also include references to scientific or historical knowledge – in short, anything that relies on the audience's knowledge beyond the text. Intertextual references, too, can be considered to be a form of cultural code in that they reference meanings from outside the product. Tide, for instance, offers cultural coding through the intertextual reference made to the 'We can do it' Second World War propaganda poster (Figure 1.3). The reference here constructs the suggestion that Tide is a patriotic product.

Figure 1.3 'We Can Do It!' American Second World War propaganda poster (1943).

Source: image courtesy of Advertising Archive.

Box 1.2 Apply it: apply Barthes's five code symphony to set texts

Work through set texts that require an understanding of the effects of media language. Identify how each text crafts hermeneutic, proairetic, semantic, cultural and symbolic codes to create meaning.

Further set text help is available for a range of products for all exam boards at www.essentialmediatheory.com

---

Concept 2: the media's ideological effect

Media as myth

Traditional myths, Barthes tells us, are important because they present a collective representation of the world. Myths have an elevated status; they are important enough to be passed down from one generation to the next, while the anonymisation of their authors further suggests that mythic tales represent a collective rather than a singular view. Myths, too, are allegorical – they present moral outlooks and tell us how we ought to behave. When, for instance, Narcissus falls in love with his own reflection, we, too, are being warned about the dangers of vanity and self-absorption.

Barthes suggests that the media has replaced, or at least replicates, the functions of traditional myth making. The press, television, advertising and radio, he argues, convey meaning with the same sort of authority as myths and, more, importantly, induce similar ideological effects.

Indeed, Barthes's hugely influential essay collection, *Mythologies*, sought to identify those mythic effects, suggesting that advertising invests cars with a godlike spirituality, that politicians manufacture imagery to convince us of their ordinariness and that soap detergents effect a 'euphoria' of cleanliness through their marketing appeals (Barthes, 2009, 32).

Barthes identifies the following ideological effects of media consumption:

- **Naturalisation:** as a result of the media's uncanny ability to look and feel realistic, media products, Barthes tells us, present ideas as natural, matter of fact or common sense. Indeed, if a range of media texts repeat the same idea enough times audiences come to believe that those ideas are not a matter of perspective but are, in fact, an immutable social norm. For instance, advertising that positions women as mothers or as responsible for domestic chores naturalise the idea that a woman's place ought to be in the home.

• **Media myths are reductive:** Barthes tells us that the media, by and large, simplifies, reduces or purifies ideas, turning complexity into easily digestible information. The use of simplicity creates audience appeal, Barthes argues, and also has the effect of de-intellectualising and depoliticising ideas. Message reduction also discourages audiences from questioning or analysing media content too closely.

• **Media myths reinforce existing social power structures:** 'The oppressed is nothing, he has only one language, that of his emancipation,' Barthes writes, while 'the oppressor is everything, his language is rich, multiform, supple' (Barthes, 2009, 176). He argues that those who have power tend to control the myth-making process, either owning or indirectly channelling media content through privileged access arrangements. The powerful, in this sense, hold all the cards, and are able to harness the creative allure of the media industry to maintain the illusion that the system we live in, the system that benefits the powerful the most, is naturally ordered and unchangeable.

Box 1.3 Discuss it: what effect do media products have on society?

• Can you think of a media product that consistently turns complexity into a simplified or reductive message?
• Do any of your set texts deploy message reduction? Why?
• Can you think of an idea, behaviour or norm that the media naturalises?
• Are modern audiences more suspicious of the media than Barthes suggests?
• Do media products reinforce existing power structures? Can you think of any media products that challenge those who have power?

Box 1.4 Apply it: diagnose the ideological subtexts of your set texts

Use the following questions to help you identify the ideological subtexts of set text products:

• **Naturalisation effects:** in what ways does the set text present key ideas, values or behaviours as common sense or the norm?

• **Simplification effects:** in what ways does the text create appeal for those ideas through a simplistic presentation? How does that simplicity discourage audience questioning?

• **Reinforcement of existing power structures:** who has power within the set text? How does that power mirror real world power?

Exemplar analysis and further set text help is available for a range of products at www.essentialmediatheory.com

---

Table 1.2 Speak Roland Barthes

Anchorage	The process of fixing the meaning, usually the meaning of an image, through the use of another component – usually a text-based feature such as a header or caption.
Denotation/ connotation	Denotation refers to the literal meaning of a media element, whilst connotation refers to the emotions, ideas or symbolic meanings produced by that element.
Hermeneutic codes	Hermeneutic elements construct mystery or enigma, encouraging the reader to engage further with a product in order to discover the answer to the puzzle posed.
Naturalisation	The process of making ideas or viewpoints feel like they are common sense when, in reality, they are constructed or manufactured by media producers.
Message reduction	Barthes argues that the media tends to simplify or purify complex ideas. This reductive impulse discourages audiences from questioning the ideas presented.
Proairetic codes	Refers to moments of action within a media text. Proairetic moments create excitement or provide explanation for audiences.
Signification	The process of meaning creation. Media elements signify or produce meanings when consumed by audiences.

Table 1.3 Barthes: ten minute revision

Concept 1: *the media constructs meaning through a process of denotation and connotation*

- We read the media imagery in the same way that we read conventional language.
- We decode media imagery in two distinctly different ways: first, producing a denotative reading that recognises the literal content of an image, and then producing a connotative reading that diagnoses a deeper symbolic meaning.
- Image based connotations are created through: props, post-production effects, pose, costuming, composition and lighting.
- Media imagery is polyvalent – likely, in other words, to produce a number of connotative effects.
- Text-based elements can provide anchorage – tying down the meaning of an image for the reader.
- Barthes suggests that meaning is produced by the simultaneous deployment of hermeneutic, proairetic, semantic, cultural and symbolic features.

Concept 2: *the media has an ideological effect on audiences*

- The media is powerful because it has the capacity to produce a realistic portrayal of the world.
- The media has a myth like capacity to guide and influence our behaviours and actions.
- The media naturalises ideas through repetition.
- The media reduces or simplifies ideas, discouraging audiences from questioning its specific presentation of the world.
- The media tends to reinforce the worldview of those who affect social power.

Two theorists who challenge Barthes's thinking

- **Claude Lévi-Strauss:** would be more interested in the way that media products articulate oppositions than in the effect of any single ingredient or moment. Lévi-Strauss would also argue that media products are informed by universally shared structures; Barthes argues that media products are constructed as a result of temporal or social influences.
- **Tzvetan Todorov:** would argue that media products produce meaning through narrative features and that isolated instances of connotation are less significant.

2   Structuralism

Claude Lévi-Strauss

Lévi-Strauss painstakingly analysed the structure and narrative content of hundreds of mythic tales he collected from around the globe. From the tribal stories of the Amazonian rainforest to the ancient myths of Greece, he sought to uncover the invisible rule book of storytelling in order to diagnose the essential nature of human experience; he believed that any common themes or motifs located in those myths would reveal essential truths about the way the human mind structures the world.

All stories, Lévi-Strauss ultimately concluded, work through oppositional arrangements – through the construction of characters or narrative incidents that clash or jar. Moreover, stories and storytelling, in Lévi-Strauss's view, perform a vital social function: oppositional presentations are resolved to outline societal taboos and socially acceptable behaviours.

Concept 1: binary oppositions

Lévi-Strauss outlines the key academic ideas used to explore media products in his 1962 book, *The Savage Mind*, in which he suggests that a subliminal set of structural rules inform myth production. Individual cultures might speak different languages, Lévi-Strauss argues, but all stories told across the globe and throughout history employ a remarkably simple but stable formula. Myths, Lévi-Strauss infers, universally explore human experience using polarised themes: birth has to compete against death, success against failure, wisdom trades blows with innocence. The Old Testament, for instance, suggests that the Earth was formed from a series of oppositional constructs – God separated light from darkness, the sky from the sea, the land from the water. In fairy tales, the innocence and youth of Little Red Riding Hood takes on the greed and cunning of the Big Bad Wolf.

Lévi-Strauss infers further that the universal use of these oppositional forces to organise stories is prompted by humankind's innate bias towards organising the world using binary thinking. Pre-modern man's need to distinguish poisonous from edible foodstuffs, Lévi-Strauss argues, embedded a cognitive blueprint that directs human beings to read the world using oppositional descriptors.

Humans do not do ambiguity, Lévi-Strauss tells us. We simplify the world around us using an age-old bias towards binary thinking. Certainly, binary labels and binary thinking are evidenced aplenty in today's complex world. We continue to label ourselves as female or male, masculine or feminine, despite the multiplicity of gender choices at play in Western society. Similarly, our political governance is polarised as left or right wing, while human morality is packaged up in deeds that are categorised as good or evil, saintly or sinful.

Media based binary oppositions

Lévi-Strauss did not allude to the structure of contemporary media products directly, but if we buy into the idea that binary thinking is a universal feature of storytelling then it stands to reason that media narratives are organised using the same structural blueprints as those offered in myths. Oppositions in media products might be inferred through the following:

• **Character oppositions:** audiences expect villains to battle heroes. Oppositions, too, might also centre on secondary characters, with contrasts constructed in terms of youth or maturity, strength or

---

Box 2.1 Think about it: do humans organise the world using binary thinking?

Can you think of any further evidence that would reinforce the idea that humans naturally organise the world using simplified binaries?

• What kinds of media products are particularly prone to using binary oppositions?

• In what ways do your set texts use oppositions?

• Do any of your set texts resist the use of simple binary oppositions?

intelligence, masculinity or femininity. Character oppositions can be found in real world products too: newspapers deploy stories in which criminals exploit victims, while documentaries depict innocent subjects who fall prey to anonymous corporations.

• **Narrative oppositions:** media stories, too, are organised to construct moments of opposition. Print and television advertising, for instance, transforms failure into success through simplified binary presentations. Television narratives conventionally culminate in a grand narrative collision so that they might deliver a finale of story excitement for their audiences.

• **Stylistic oppositions:** media producers also encode products using juxtaposed stylistic presentations. Camera work might change from quiet stasis in one scene to a frenzied set of whip pans in another. Transitions of this kind can reinforce wider character-oriented oppositions or are deployed to create aesthetic interest. Table 2.1 identifies some of the common stylistic oppositions used by contemporary media texts.

• **Genre-driven binary oppositions:** some binary oppositions are so deeply entrenched within genres that they become a convention or expectation of that genre. Science fiction products, for instance, regularly offer audiences 'technology versus humanity' driven narratives; crime dramas routinely deploy 'law enforcer/law breaker' character stereotypes; romances resolve in romantic couplings.

Box 2.2 Apply it: diagnose genre-driven oppositions in your set texts

Use Table 2.3 at the end of this chapter to identify the genre-driven oppositions present within the set texts you are studying. Think about the following questions to help you add further detail:

• Which thematic oppositions are presented by your set texts?
• How do the characters in your set texts reflect those oppositions?
• How do stylistic/design decisions used within those set texts reflect the character oppositions presented? Think in terms of: camera work, *mise en scène* sound, editing, language or imagery usage, typography and layout.

Exemplar analysis and further set text help is available for a range of products at www.essentialmediatheory.com

The function of oppositions in media products

Media makers, moreover, deploy binary oppositions to create a range of audience-oriented effects. The potential functions of binary oppositions in contemporary storytelling are used for the following reasons:

• **To clearly explain ideas.** Binary oppositions can be used to simplify viewpoints or make complicated ideas understandable for viewers and readers. News stories, for instance, often explain complex topics by referencing interviewees with oppositional viewpoints to generate simplified overviews.

• **To create compelling narratives.** The inclusion of binary oppositions inevitably creates conflict. Audiences are more likely to engage with a media product if they are presented with the promise of a narrative clash.

• **To create identifiable character types.** Audiences can quickly gain a sense of the direction of a story once oppositional characters are introduced – we implicitly understand that the hero has to fight the villain or that the good guy will win over his girl. The use of clashing characters can also produce a range of other gratifications – comedy, fear and so on.

• **To create audience identification.** Binary oppositions prompt audiences to identify with one central character or viewpoint. An advert, for instance, that contrasts humdrum reality with the sparkle of an advertised product clearly positions the audience to empathise with the brand promoted.

Box 2.3 Revise it: prepare your own stylistics analysis paragraphs

This exercise will take lots of time to execute, but ought to help produce detailed responses that can be adapted for a huge variety of exam questions. Use Table 2.1 and the following prompts to help you develop your responses:

Relating stylistic oppositions to wider themes

• In what ways do stylistic oppositions reinforce genre-oriented expectations?
• In what ways do stylistic oppositions narrate the wider themes of the set text?

- What messages do the oppositions used convey to audiences?

Stylistic analysis prompts

- Are there moments where locations, props or costuming contrast? Why have they been styled this way?
- Are colour contrasts offered in your set texts and to what effect?
- How do editing, camera or lighting styles change across the time-lines of your set texts? How do these stylistic oppositions support wider narrative themes?
- Do sound elements offer significant moments of contrast in terms of volume, tone, key signatures or instrumentation? What effect do these aural contrasts have on audiences?

Exemplar: Old Spice (OCR). The benefits of using Old Spice in the set text Bahamas advert are conveyed through a series of Straussian binary oppositions. The calm composure of the central model is juxta-posed with the chaotic activity taking place beneath him – for instance, fishermen struggle to land their catches, while a ship sinks comically behind the model. A contrasting colour palette is similarly deployed with the orange heat of the volcano setting provoking a deliberate con-trast with the idyllic blue sky above. These stylised features combine to construct a 'calm' versus 'chaos' binary, prompting the product's audi-ence to understand that Old Spice facilitates composure under stressful conditions.

Exemplar: WaterAid (Eduqas). WaterAid underlines the contrasting experiences of the advert's UK audience with those experiencing water poverty in Africa. A carefully choreographed set of stylistic oppositions at the start of the advert reinforces this sentiment, with the opening shot of a rain-soaked British scene (composed as a claustrophobic closed framed composition) providing a stark contrast to the open-framed depiction of Claudia's sun-soaked village. Aurally, too, the rainy ambi-ence of the first scene is replaced by the arid crunch of Claudia's foot-steps, while the green colour palettes of Britain transform into dusty browns of the African savannah. These stylistic clashes are used, ulti-mately, to underline the stark disparities that exist between the viewers' water rich existence and those less fortunate than themselves.

Further exemplar paragraphs for set texts from all exam boards are available at www.essentialmediatheory.com

Table 2.1 Common stylistic oppositions used within media texts

Camera	Open/closed framing Left/right frame composition Left/right tracking Up/down tilt Thin/thick depth of field Static/handheld movement Extreme close up/long shot	**Sound**	Loud/soft volume High/low pitched instrumentation Minor key/major key score String/brass timbre Agitated/calm room tone Ascending/descending shepherd tones
Editing	Slow/fast editing rhythm Stretched/elliptical edits Continuity/montage editing Straight cut/dissolve transitions Long takes/jump cutting Saturated/desaturated edit	***Mise en scène***	Low/high key lighting Warm/cold lighting Realistic/escapist *mise en scène* Lifeless/animated body language Real/ideal costuming Sunny/stormy weather

Concept 2: binary oppositions and ideological significance

Myths, according to Lévi-Strauss, articulate a version of the world around us, generating culturally specific cues that define acceptable or unacceptable social norms. Those cues, Lévi-Strauss infers, are created as a result of the way that story oppositions resolve – in the way that select oppositions are disregarded in favour of their counterparts. Narratives, in this sense, provide audiences with a set of privileged behaviours or ideals that they are encouraged to copy or adopt.

Lévi-Strauss proposes, for instance, that a principle function of primitive myth was to describe incest taboos and the rules of marriage. For example, Sophocles famous Oedipus myth, Lévi-Strauss explains, illustrates the dangers of unnatural sexual relationships. The binary oppositions constructed in the story, he suggests, centre on the masculine energy of Oedipus and the femininity of Oedipus's mother. Famously, Oedipus blinds himself when he discovers he has accidentally married his own mother – Oedipus's shame in transgressing natural incest taboos is so deeply felt that he can longer bear to look upon the world. The resolution of the male/female oppositions presented, Levi-Strauss explains, convey a clear warning to the myth's readers and listeners – don't have sex with your own mother.

Likewise, cultural products – art, literature and the media – do not just present conflict in their narratives; they offer resolutions to those oppositions. In film, for instance, protagonists invariably win their battles. James Bond always crushes the terrorist plot. The Avengers inevitably destroy their seemingly undefeatable enemies, while the supernatural presence that terrorises us in horror films is terminally exorcised in time for the end credits to roll.

Narratives resolve oppositions, and that resolution process allows media products to play a significant role in promoting an explicit set of values and ideologies. James Bond's triumph over the forces of evil, for example, privileges a quintessential sense of Britishness. 007 not only fights bad guys, he reinstates democracy, moral decency and English tradition at the expense of totalitarianism, capitalist greed or religious fanaticism.

Oppositional resolutions in news products

The news, too, resolves stories in a manner that privileges one set of oppositions. Newspapers teach us that criminals are caught, that corrupt politicians lose elections, or that wayward celebrities have to endure rehab hell. The news does not just represent the chaos of the world, nor does it merely order that chaos into neat binaries – news stories are crafted in ways that reinforce cultural or editorial biases, and the resolutions that publications craft privilege those cultural biases to their readerships.

A news product reporting a terrorist attack, for instance, might outline the suffering and death inflicted by the incident, but those losses are often offset by coverage that emphasises the everyday acts of heroism that surround the incident. Police officers and fire crews step into the fray when bombers attack, innocent members of the public sacrifice themselves to save others and, when the terrorist dust has settled, the incident news cycle inevitably concludes with follow-ups that articulate the ongoing solidarity and defiance of the communities affected by the bombing. Yes, the news articulates oppositions to create conflict and to sell more editions, yet, much like fictional media, news narratives construct resolutions to forward editorial viewpoints and to reinforce cultural norms. Table 2.2 further outlines the uses and purposes of binary oppositions by print news and a range of other media forms. Use Table 2.3 to help you uncover the narrative oppositions presented by your set texts.

Box 2.4 Revise it: prepare your own set text resolution analysis paragraphs

Lévi-Strauss's ideas concerning narrative resolution can be used to determine the underlying ideological significance of a media product. Most media products give an uneven presentation of oppositional conflicts, positioning their audiences to agree with one set of ideas at the expense of other oppositions. Use the following questions to construct power paragraphs that define the character, genre or stylistic oppositions constructed by set texts and to reach conclusions as to the ideological viewpoints that are privileged.

Genre/narrative resolutions

• Use Table 2.3 to identify the genre-based oppositions created. Which of the oppositions triumph in the set text? Where and how?

• How do narratives end? Do the resolutions offered at the end of stories tell us anything about the ideological subtexts of your set texts?

Character resolutions

• How does characterisation produce conflict?
• Have the product's authors crafted oppositional characters?
• How are audiences positioned to empathise with specific characters?
• Which characters triumph in the product and with what ideological effect?

Exemplar paragraph: Common, *Letter to the Free* (AQA). Common's music video replicates many of the genre-driven oppositions constructed by politically aware hip-hop musicians. *Letter to the Free's* black and white aesthetic, for instance, reduces the product's visual appearance to a sombre two-tone colour palette that explores black oppression in white America. The physical oppression of black America is further represented via the prison setting. Yet the jazz musicians of the video offer resistance, flaunting the 'no excessive noise' notice to articulate a 'freedom versus restraint' Straussian binary; and although the video consists almost entirely of claustrophobic closed frame compositions and is lit using a low-key lighting style, the final scene offers some sense of hope – inverting the black and white aesthetic in a final open framed composition to proffer the conclusion that black freedom is both possible and inevitable.

Further set text help is available for a range of products for all exam boards at www.essentialmediatheory.com

Table 2.2 Binary oppositions in different media: uses and applications revision overview

Form	Where to look for oppositions	Reasons for use
News, magazines	• **Opposing viewpoints** of different commentators and interviewees. • Within **imagery** that depicts oppositional characteristics. • **Language** might use oppositional semantic fields or contrasting lexical styles. • **Profile pieces** are likely to present conflict outlining the barriers and binary choices that interviewees have had to overcome.	• To explain and simplify complex issues. • To position audiences so that they identify with the editorial stance of the paper. • To construct an emotional response from the audience. • To construct crisis-driven stories that offer conflict and enigma.
Film marketing, gaming, television, music video	• **Character construction:** look beyond simple antagonist and protagonist oppositions. Think about age, gender and class-based oppositions offered via secondary characters. • **Mise en scène:** Costumes, locations, body language and colour palettes are likely to offer juxtapositions to support the wider themes of narratives or to identify character conflict. • **Narrative events:** identify story points that can be ordered as oppositional – repeated sequences or moments that use cross-cutting are likely to offer visible oppositions.	• To create compelling narratives that offer conflict. • To outline overarching narrative themes. • To produce oppositions that enable the product to be recognisable as genre driven.
Advertising	• **Narrative construction.** Classic binary story structures in adverts include: before and after product use, non-ideal/ideal lifestyle positioning, problem/solution product positioning. • **Mise en scène:** costumes, locations, body language and colour palettes are likely to be juxtaposed to support the wider themes of the product.	• To enable speedy character identification. • To create simplified narratives that justify product needs. • To enable audiences to understand the advantages of using a product in terms of the lifestyle advantages it could bring.

Table 2.3 Common oppositions found with genres and forms that are popular within the contemporary media landscape

Music video	News	Magazines
Desire/rejection	Chaos/order	Freedom/control
Loss/belonging	Green issues/economics	Happiness/responsibility
Love/loneliness	Justice/injustice	Health/illness
Masculinity/femininity	Left wing/right wing	Loss/belonging
Nostalgia/reality	Poverty/greed	Love/loss
Oppression/freedom	Power/powerlessness	Masculinity/femininity
Rebellion/authority	Society/the individual	Romance/lust
Youth/authority	Victims/perpetrators	Work/leisure
Science fiction	**Crime/politics**	**Horror**
Aliens/humans	Chaos/order	Chaos/order
Corporate power/	Choice/necessity	Darkness/light
individualism	Corruption/innocence	Death/life
Exploitation/freedom	Freedom/duty	Good/evil
Knowledge/ignorance	Guilt/innocence	Known/unknown
Machine/man	Law/justice	Past/present
Man/nature	Lawfulness/lawlessness	Reality/supernatural
Reality/deception	Morality/greed	Reason/madness
Technology/humanity	Power/weakness	Religion/disbelief
	Self-interest/society	Repression/acceptance
Romance	**War**	**Spy/thriller**
Experience/youth	Allies/enemies	Democracy/tyranny
Family ties/romance	Duty/morality	Heroism/greed
Friendship/betrayal	Experience/innocence	Hunter/hunted
Loneliness/belonging	Family/duty	Intellect/action
Masculinity/femininity	Home front/the front line	Order/chaos
Relationships/freedom	Honour/self-interest	Patriotism/treachery
Romance/money	Sacrifice/self interest	State/individual
	Survival/patriotism	Surveillance/subterfuge

Table 2.4 Speak Claude Lévi-Strauss

Binary oppositions	The use of paired elements within a narrative that provide contrast.
Character oppositions	The construction of characters that are juxtaposed – oppositions might be based on age, ability, moral outlook or social position.
Genre-based oppositions	Paired elements that are commonly found in specific genres – these might be character, narrative or theme-based oppositions.
Opposition resolution	Refers to the way that binary opposites resolve within a narrative – the dominant partner in an oppositional arrangement will often dictate the ideological position of a media product.
Structuralism	An analytical model that suggests that human behaviour is directed by a universally applicable set of rules. Lévi-Strauss's suggestion that humans naturally explain the world in terms of oppositions is a structuralist argument.
Stylistic oppositions	The use of contrasting design elements. Stylistic oppositions often reinforce the narrative themes of a text or help encode character oppositions.

Table 2.5 Lévi-Strauss: ten minute revision

Concept 1: *media narratives use binary oppositions*
- Lévi-Strauss offers a structuralist approach to media analysis, suggesting that humans encode and decode the world using universally shared principles.
- The media uses binary oppositions to explain and categorise the complexities of the world around us.
- Oppositions can be found in the media in the presentation of characters or narrative themes.
- Media makers also apply stylistic oppositions to *mise en scène*, camera work, editing styles and image construction.
- Thematic oppositions in media products can be genre driven.

Concept 2: *the way binary oppositions are resolved creates ideological significance*
- Media products construct ideologies by positioning their audiences to favour one side of an opposition.
- Narrative resolutions – the endings of media products – often help us to diagnose which oppositions a product favours.

Three theorists who challenge Lévi-Strauss's thinking
- **Stuart Hall:** would also argue that media products can be encoded using binary oppositions, but he would add that audiences do not necessarily decode the products in the way that media makers intend.
- **Paul Gilroy:** argues that Western binary thinking has traditionally classified ethnicity in terms of simplified white/non-white and civilised/uncivilised categories. He calls for the media to move beyond these simplistic and hugely damaging binary classifications.
- **Judith Butler:** similarly argues that conventional Western gender binaries mask the complex nature of sexuality. She also argues that individuals have resisted gender binary using 'gender trouble'.

3 Narratology

Tzvetan Todorov

Todorov, like Lévi-Strauss, was interested in the possibility that all stories share similar narrative features, and that, if we can understand and detect those features, we can better comprehend the hidden meanings that media texts present to their audiences. The crucial difference between Todorov and Lévi-Strauss, however, lies in the former theorist's assertion that stories do not just construct oppositions, but that characters and ideas are transformed by oppositional forces. More importantly, the recognition of those transformations by audiences creates moments of ideological instruction, prompting readers and viewers to transform their own real world behaviours.

Concept 1: the three act ideal

The influence of Vladimir Propp

Todorov was hugely influenced by the Russian literary theorist Vladimir Propp and his highly influential 1929 book, *Morphology of the Folktale*, in which Propp famously analysed hundreds of Russian folk stories in an attempt to uncover their underlying narrative structures. Importantly, Propp arrived at the conclusion that folk tales drew from a highly stable list of characters whose roles and narrative functions he defined as follows (Propp, 2009):

- **The hero:** Propp identifies two significant types of hero – the seeker-hero (who relies more heavily on the donor to perform their quest) and the victim-hero (who needs to overcome a weakness to complete their quest).

- **The villain:** fights or pursues the hero and must be defeated if the hero is to accomplish their quest.
- **The princess and the princess's father:** the princess usually represents the reward of the hero's quest, while the princess's father often sets the hero difficult tasks to prevent them from marrying the princess.
- **The donor:** provides the hero with a magical agent that allows the hero to defeat the villain.
- **The helper:** usually accompanies the hero on their quest, saving them from the struggles encountered on their journey, helping them to overcome the difficult tasks encountered on their quest.
- **The dispatcher:** sends the hero on his or her quest, usually at the start of the story.
- **The false hero:** performs a largely villainous role, usurping the true hero's position in the course of the story. The false hero is usually unmasked in the last act of a narrative.

Propp suggested that stories do not necessarily have to use all the characters listed, though most are organised around the interplay of the hero, villain and princess archetypes. Propp also discovered that the fairy stories he analysed followed a remarkably similar narrative structure, organised using a combination of just 31 closely defined plot moments that he called 'narratemes'. The starting points of most stories (narratemes 1–7) usually introduce, he observed, the hero and other key characters. The villain, Propp tells us, usually appears at narrateme 4, prompting the hero to embark on their quest and culminating in the hero's final struggle with the villain at narrateme 26. Propp suggests that stories do not necessarily have to be composed of all 31 narratemes, but those that are used are relayed in strict linear fashion. See Table 3.1 for a further outline of the narrative progression Propp identified in *Morphology of the Folktale*.

Todorov's refinement of Propp's narrative theory

Todorov refined Propp's narrative theory in the 1970s, arguing that media narratives are created using moments of action, or as Todorov called them 'propositions', and that those moments combine into narrative sequences. Broadly speaking, Todorov also argued that narratives tend to follow similar patterns; that the start of any story is concerned, largely, with the outlining of characters in stable worlds, while later

Table 3.1 Key narrative moments – as described in Propp's *Morphology of the Folktale*

Movement	Narrative stage	Potential plot points
First movement	**The initial situation**	• The hero's home life is described.
	The preparatory section	• The false hero is introduced. • The hero faces a significant barrier that disrupts their home life. • The hero is deceived by the villain. • The hero uncovers the deception.
	The complication	• The villain's influence increases and/or the princess is captured. • The hero's quest is defined and they are dispatched on a journey to complete that quest.
	The donor	• Appearance of the donor character who provides a magic agent so that the hero can complete their quest.
	The helper	• The hero faces struggles that they overcome with the assistance of the helper. • The hero does battle with the villain for the first time. • The false hero wins favour with the father of the princess. • The hero pursues the villain.
Second movement	**Repetition**	• The hero continues to battle the villain using both the donor and helper's assistance • The hero continues to face barriers that prevent the completion of their quest.
	The difficult task	• The hero engages in a final struggle with the villain. • The false hero is unmasked. • The hero is recognised as the true hero. • The world is transfigured. • The false hero is punished. • The hero marries the princess.

Box 3.1 Think about it: the use of Proppian character/ narrative archetypes in contemporary media products

Many would argue that Propp's analysis is equally applicable to contemporary media products. Think about the following questions:

• Can you think of any media products that use Propp's character archetypes?
• Can you think of any media products that use a similar structure to that defined in Table 3.1?
• Do you enjoy watching media products that follow this structure? Why or why not?

---

sequences offer challenges to that stability. Like Propp, Todorov also highlighted the importance of character transformation within a story. Characters do not just experience adversity; they are transformed by those experiences.

Todorov suggests, as a result, that an 'ideal' narrative is organised using the following story structure (Todorov, 1977, 111):

• **Equilibrium:** the story constructs a stable world at the outset of the narrative. Key characters are presented as part of that stability.
• **Disruption:** Oppositional forces − the actions of a villain, perhaps, or some kind of calamity − destabilise the story's equilibrium. Lead protagonists attempt to repair the disruption caused.
• **New equilibrium:** disruption is repaired and stability restored. Importantly, the equilibrium achieved at the end of the story is different to that outlined at the start. The world is transformed.

Todorovian three act narratives are used to structure stories across a range of media: from Hollywood film to television drama, the equilibrium/disequilibrium/transformation formula provides the narrative backbone for a great deal of the screen-based fiction we consume (see Table 3.2 for further examples). Three act narratives, too, are used in print storytelling: celebrity interviews, for instance, are structured using moments of disequilibrium and repair − alcoholism, the difficulties of producing a film and marriage break-ups are used to construct moments of narrative disequilibrium. Three act narratives are universally

Table 3.2 Examples of Todorov's ideal narrative formula in popular TV drama genres

Genre	Equilibrium	Disruption	New Equilibrium
Science fiction	The world is at peace. A dysfunctional family recovers from a messy divorce.	Aliens land. The family have to survive and are drawn into a battle to save the planet.	The aliens are defeated. The family is healed – the separated parents are reunited.
Horror	An ordinary family home – teenagers fight with their parents.	A supernatural force takes over the home.	The supernatural entity is banished. The teenagers and parents learn to respect one another.
Romance	Single girl yearns for romance. The girl is also stuck in a dead-end job that she hates.	The girl falls in love with a bad guy who leads her astray.	The bad guy is ditched and the girl finds her true love. She also sets up a successful business.

present in factual programming too: the loveless subjects of Channel 4's *The Undateables* find true romance, criminal disruptions are repaired in *24 Hours in Police Custody*, while Netflix's *Queer Eye* team heal the broken lives of American singletons across the United States. In their simplest form, traditional three act narratives are typically delivered to audiences using the following features:

*   **Stories are linear:** conventionally, three act narratives move forward in time, progressing through Todorov's equilibrium, disequilibrium and new equilibrium formula using successive narrative events.
*   **Proppian character stereotypes are used:** in their purest form, Todorovian narratives tend to use conventional Proppian archetypes, clustering around heroes, princesses and villains.
*   **Single character transformations are pursued:** traditional Todorovian story arcs habitually place one lead hero at the centre of the story. Secondary characters, Proppian helpers, false heroes and so on are deployed to assist that single central hero in their narrative quest.

A more sophisticated application of Todorov

Todorov, importantly, recognises that stories are constructed in ways that test and subvert the three act narrative structure outlined above. Stories, he acknowledges, can wholly omit equilibrium or disruption stages. A more sophisticated application of Todorov might also consider:

*   **Plot and subplot(s):** contemporary film and television drama is traditionally constructed using an overarching master plot accompanied by a series of subplots. Each of these narrative layers will articulate their own individual equilibrium, disequilibrium and transformation sequences.
*   **Multiple equilibrium/disruption sequences:** contemporary media products often try to produce a roller-coaster effect for their audiences by deploying several equilibrium/disequilibrium sequences before resolving in a final transformation. The alternating repose/action effect of such narratives offers audiences multiple moments of narrative calm and excitement.
*   **Flexi-narratives:** long format television products deploy multiple three act structures in a similar pattern to that used by master plot/

subplot sequences, with some narratives resolved in a single episode and others concluded over the course of a whole season or even longer in some instances. These flexible narratives offer audiences quick fix single episode resolutions, while also nurturing long-term viewing engagement by building season long three act arcs.

• **Condensed equilibriums:** contemporary audiences, arguably, have a much lower boredom threshold, expecting products to deliver action or disruption quickly. Producers therefore propel narratives towards moments of immediate disruption to hook audience engagement from the outset.

Alternative story ordering devices

Audience demand for story novelty has encouraged writers and directors to test the three act narrative formula in ever more ingenious ways. Indeed, today's media saturated landscape means that consumers skim across products at the tap of their remote controls or the swipe of a tablet screen, compelling contemporary storytellers to create ever faster product engagement. The accelerated, multifaceted nature of media consumption is also reflected in the construction of ever more complex narratives that are not afraid to test the linear rules of storytelling.

Stories move backwards and forwards. They skip or recap, they start at the end, and end at the start.

Contemporary viewers, moreover, shift their attention continuously: from TV screens to tablets, from tablets to smartphones, watching and listening to two or more products simultaneously. And audiences do not wait for their media to appear in fixed schedule broadcasting slots. Consumption is slaked in binge watching gulps or, conversely, is nibbled upon in YouTube friendly 15 minute snacks. In short, contemporary audiences expect more of the narratives they engage with, while the complex consumption habits of those audiences suitably equip them to successfully decode products that bend or refashion Todorov's ideal formula. These are some of the contemporary narrative strategies used that test or break the traditional rules of media storytelling:

• **Anachronic devices (flash forward/flashback):** subvert traditional linear storytelling techniques through time bending. Flash forwards provide moments of disequilibrium before equilibrium – reversing Todorov's ideal flow by telling us the end of the story before it has begun. Flashbacks, too, are injected to disrupt the highly predictable nature of the three act structure.

Box 3.2 Apply it: in what ways can the Todorov formula be applied to your set texts?

Use the following questions to help you explore the use of equilibrium/ disequilibrium sequences in your set texts.

- Do the set texts use Proppian character types?
- Do products use Todorov's equilibrium, disequilibrium and transformation formula?
- Do products revolve around one lead character?
- Do the set text products provide plot/subplot sequences? Flexi-narratives?
- Do the set texts condense or shorten equilibriums?
- Do stories resolve narrative strands at different points across the text?
- In what ways are lead characters transformed in new equilibrium stages?
- In what ways are Propp and Todorov's ideas tested by your set texts?

Exemplar: *No Offence* (AQA). *No Offence* simultaneously applies and adapts Todorov's ideal narrative formula. The opening sequence of season two offers us a compressed sense of equilibrium – reintroducing the audience to the main characters of the narrative and their character quirks. The lead hero, Viv, is identified immediately with secondary team members (Dinah and Joy) positioned as her Proppian helpers. The opening scene presents a brief moment of compressed equilibrium – outlining the dysfunctional nature of the team via Joy's indiscretion in the surveillance van, while Viv's exposed fashion label reinforces the hero's lack of traditional femininity. Equilibrium, however, quickly gives way to 'in media res' – the terrorist explosion producing a quick narrative hook for the audience while also engaging viewers in a narrative arc that unfolds across the whole of season two. *No Offence*, in this sense, is best defined as a contemporary flexi-narrative, as opposed to offering its audience a traditional Todorovian three act structure.

Further set text help is available for a range of products at www.essentialmedia theory.com

---

- **In media res:** contemporary stories often start mid-action, delivering immediate crisis, inverting Todorov's ideal narrative progression through the presentation of disequilibrium before equilibrium.

- **Multiperspective narratives:** contemporary stories are often told from different character perspectives, repurposing equilibriums as disequilibrium when the story shifts from one character viewpoint to another.

- **Metanarratives:** provide audiences with moments that draw attention to the idea that they are watching a story. Metanarration might knowingly refer to the product as a media construct or speak directly to audiences through fourth wall breaks.

- **Unreliable narration:** deliberately deceive audiences, providing plots that deliver unexpected moments – usually by revealing that a character is not who they claim to be.

- **Frame stories:** stories told inside of stories, testing Todorov's ideal narrative structure through the presentation of nested moments of equilibrium and disequilibrium.

Concept 2: the ideological effects of story structure

Stories, Todorov suggests, invite audiences to interpret meanings – to decode the presentation of characters and narrative action as substitutes for ideas that exist beyond immediate plot presentations. 'An adventure,' he writes, 'is *at the same time* a real adventure and the symbol of another adventure' (Todorov, 1977, 127). Stories, Todorov tells us, are metaphors – places where contradictory forces can do battle, where human desires can be articulated and curtailed. Stories, too, provide collisions, delineating harmony and disruption, and, in this sense, their effect upon the reader is both persuasive and ideological.

Todorov draws attention to the following ways in which narratives construct symbolic meaning:

- **Narratives are significations.** Even though narratives are set within reality, the construction of that reality is symbolic – offering us a version of the world that is ordered by the ethical, moral or ideological viewpoints of a text's author.

- **Stories articulate desire.** Todorov's 'ideal' narrative structure is often underlined by the desire of lead characters to return to the stable world presented during the initial equilibrium stage. Moments of initial equilibrium, therefore, represent ideals for the audience watching the text.

- **Stories invoke desire:** story quests, the journeys taken by lead characters, are also motivated by the desire to change – to move beyond the initial circumstances in which a character is placed. That journey, Todorov suggests, prompts the reader to change too.
- **Disequilibrium and transgression:** Todorov identifies the use of transgressive action as a mechanism that also enables ideological meanings to form. Characters break rules or violate social norms and to repair those transgressions they must be punished or effect a transformation. The ideological effect of these moments is to outline social ideals or modes of behaviour that audiences might also use to guide their own behaviours.
- **Disequilibrium and ideological villainy:** narrative disequilibrium is also constructed through the presence and actions of symbolic villains. Here, the hero must battle an external foe, who, Todorov argues, symbolises qualities that audiences are guided to avoid.

Box 3.3 Think about it: the power of narrative transformation

Todorov argues that narrative transformation is a defining feature of fiction, differentiating stories from other modes of discourse such as factual or historical narration. Todorov suggests that stories can construct the following types of transformation:

1 **Transformation in attitude:** media products construct characters who have to develop new outlooks in order to overcome the challenges posed during disruption.
2 **Transformations of belief:** narratives outline both the ideas and ideals that we have to believe in if we are to succeed, while also outlining destructive beliefs.
3 **Transformations of knowledge:** character quests provoke heroes to uncover new forms of knowledge and to dispense with knowledge that is no longer useful.

- Can you think of any media products that construct the different types of transformation outlined above?

- What life lessons do the products identified above pass on to their audiences?
- What are the ideological effects of these products – what attitudes, beliefs and knowledge do they suggest the readers of these texts ought to foster?

Box 3.4 Apply it: diagnose the ideological effects of narrative transformation in your set texts

Questions to ask about equilibrium stages

- In what ways does any initial narrative stability provide ideal states?
- In what ways does the narrative attempt to restore that initial harmony?

Disequilibrium effects

- Do characters produce disequilibrium by breaking social norms or rules?
- How are characters punished for those transgressions?
- What negative traits or behaviours are embodied by narrative villains?

New equilibrium effects

- Do characters affect attitude, behaviour or knowledge-based transformations?
- What do these transformations suggest?

Exemplar analysis that explore narrative transformation effects in set texts for all exam boards are available at www.essentialmediatheory.com

Table 3.3 Speak Tzvetan Todorov

Ideological effect	An ideology is a set of ideas or beliefs. Media products have an ideological effect in that they channel their audiences to believe those ideas or beliefs. Villains, for instance, might represent beliefs that are undesirable. Hero quests might also identify ideals in terms of beliefs, knowledge or behaviours.
Narrative transformation	Todorov suggests that one of the major effects of narrative lies in the way that characters or the worlds that characters inhabit are transformed at the end of a story.
Quest narrative	A narrative in which the central hero goes on a journey – usually in an attempt to repair the narrative equilibrium constructed at the start of the story.
Ideal narrative arc	Todorov suggests that the 'ideal' narrative structure follows an equilibrium, disequilibrium and new equilibrium formula. This formula is used extensively across a number of media products and forms.

Table 3.4 Todorov: ten minute revision

Concept 1: *narrative patterns – equilibrium, disequilibrium and new equilibrium*
- Todorov suggests that meaning in media products is constructed through narrative sequences and transitions rather than through any individual effect or single moment within a product.
- Todorov suggests that an ideal narrative structure follows a pattern of equilibrium, disequilibrium and new equilibrium.
- The new equilibrium stage transforms characters and the world they inhabit.

Concept 2: *the ideological effects of story structure*
- The power of stories lies in their deeper symbolic meanings.
- Narratives construct ideals for the audience through the use of equilibrium.
- Disequilibrium sequences represent ideas, values or behaviours that are deemed problematic – often these negatives ideologies are embodied through the villain character.
- Narrative transformation produces further ideals or positive models of behaviour for a media audience.

Two theorists who might challenge Todorov's thinking
- **Steve Neale:** would argue that story structures are continuously adapting and changing. The idea that there exists an 'ideal' story structure, as such, is problematic for Neale.
- **Lévi-Strauss:** is concerned with the way that narratives present oppositions rather than the way those oppositions are transformed or synthesised.

4 Genre theory

Steve Neale

Traditionally, genre-based labelling classifies products into categories or families that share common ingredients. In cinema, for instance, we usually determine whether films are best classified as westerns, horrors, melodramas, comedies, etc. but, as Steve Neale argues, genre-based categories are not fixed commodities. Genres change and subdivide, they fuse and die. Moreover, the kinds of tests we need to use to determine genre are hard to pinpoint. Is narrative structure or characterisation the principal determinant of a genre? Is a product's genre best identified by its length or by the audience-based pleasures generated?

Neale concludes that there are no fixed lists of ingredients that determine genre. Genre-driven products, he argues, create audience appeal through the repetition of some ingredients, some of the time. Indeed, products, by necessity, have to adapt genre-based formulas to maintain their commercial viability and to maximise audience engagement.

Concept 1: repetition and difference

The number of genre-based categories used to label contemporary media products have mushroomed exponentially. The growth of sub-genres and the recognition of defined genre hybrids has made the process of genre classification much more complicated than it has ever been. Indeed, what aspects of a media product might we use to even begin diagnosing the genre of a product? Neale draws our attention to the following important factors:

- **Levels of verisimilitude.** The degree to which a media product references the real world can be an incredibly useful indicator of genre. Genres that offer high levels of verisimilitude – that reference the real world with a high degree of accuracy – include news-based products, documentaries, biopics and historical drama. Conversely, genres that offer limited verisimilitude (science fiction and fantasy) transport their audiences to worlds that are escapist or fantastical.

- **Narrative similarities.** Genre-based classification can also be enabled through the identification of defined story structures or formulaic narrative devices. Murder mysteries, for instance, offer audiences the twin pleasures of suspense and surprise within their narratives. Products might also employ specific presentation techniques – news articles, for instance, start with introductory paragraphs that summarise the who, when and where of news events, while montage and flashback sequences are regularly deployed in biopics to reveal crucial backstory. The style and pace of narrative delivery might also be genre specific: voiceover narration, for example, is a staple feature of the gangster genre, while the pace and length of magazine features tends to be much slower than newsprint. Genres, too, deal in specific narrative themes or subject matter: science fiction plots often invoke 'man versus machine' plotlines; crime dramas have justice-oriented narrative themes.
- **Character-driven motifs.** Audiences expect some genres to deliver explicit character-driven motifs. Lead characters might have defined attributes or follow genre-driven narrative arcs. Crime dramas, for instance, often use anti-heroes as leads, propelling those characters on tragic narrative journeys that involve loss or redemption. Secondary character inclusion, too, might be heavily defined by genres – romances invariably contain best friend confidents; science fiction products regularly contain mad scientist character archetypes.
- **Iconography.** Iconography refers to *mise en scène* expectations (setting, costume, make-up expectations) as well as camera and editing styles. In print products, genre-driven iconography is deployed through layouts, header styles or page construction motifs. Tabloid front pages, for example, deliver high image to text ratio layouts whilst mastheads use red as their predominant colour. In film, westerns will be readily identifiable through fixed *mise en scène* expectations: guns, desert settings, horses, saloon bars, etc. will dominate the visual encodings presented to audiences.
- **Audience targeting.** Neale also highlights the way that genres are crafted to create appeal for specific audience segments. Romantic comedies are traditionally constructed to appeal to a

Box 4.1 Apply it: what conventions define the genres to which your moving image set texts belong?

Use the following questions to help you locate and determine the conventions of the genres that your moving image set texts belong to.

Verisimilitude

- Does the genre attempt to replicate or explain the real world?
- Does the genre present audiences with fantastical or otherworldly settings?

Narrative considerations

- **Structure:** What kinds of narrative structures are readily found in the genre?
- **Themes:** What binary oppositions does the genre usually deploy?
- **Narrative devices:** Does the genre use montage, flashbacks or smashed time frames? Are the narratives linear, multistrand, tragic or resolved?

Character conventions

- What stock genre-based character types occupy lead roles?
- What secondary characters do audiences expect in the genre?

Iconography

- What genre based conventions do audiences expect to see in terms of: mise en scène decisions (costume, setting, make-up), cinematography, editing styles and sound usage?

Audience appeal and representation

- For which audience is the genre traditionally constructed?
- What sorts of gender-based stereotypes does the genre deploy?

Visit www.essentialmediatheory.com to download revision flash cards that define the genre conventions for all set texts across the different exam boards.

female audience through the application of relationship-based narratives. Science fiction has traditionally created appeal for male audiences through action-based male leads.

• **Representational effects.** Neale also suggests that genres might be recognisable through their application of gender specific representations. Horror films, for instance, construct women as victims while crime dramas are conventionally led by emotionless male detectives.

Repetition and audience pleasure

The use of repeated motifs, themes or stylistic devices allows audiences to recognise and access media products that create the kinds of appeal they are engaged by. Genre-driven products also provide familiar narrative structures and character types that create audience engagement quickly. Genres, of course, also create their own specific sets of pleasures or gratifications. The appeal of science fiction lies in the construction of off-world settings. News-based products enable political engagement. Musicals provide audiences with performative pleasures through the inclusion of song and dance routines, while crime dramas traditionally provide narrative satisfaction through enigmas and surprise. In this sense, the labelling of products by media makers using genre-based categories allows audiences to identify products that generate specific pleasures or benefits.

Genre subversion

Neale resists the suggestion that genres deliver stable products for any length of time. All genres, he argues, are subject to a continuous process of evolution and/or subversion. He identifies the following drivers of that process:

• **Audience needs.** Audiences, of course, gain enjoyment from recognising the use of genre-driven tropes, but they also gain pleasure in identifying moments that depart from those expectations. These differences, Neale argues, provide moments of audience pleasure or deliver products that have unique selling points.
• **Contextual influences.** Media makers adapt genre-driven content as a result of historical, political or social influences. Social norms regarding gender-based roles, for instance, have guided a number of genres to abandon lead male character conventions.
• **Economic influences.** Falling sales or poor audience engagement can create commercial imperatives to change or adapt genre-driven

content. Similarly, budgetary constraints, or indeed budgetary freedoms, curtail or free up media makers in ways that subvert genre-based expectations. The box office success of Marvel, for instance, has led to a rapid expansion of the super-hero genre.

Box 4.2 Apply it: identify set text genre subversion

Think about the following questions to help you identify the presence of genre subversion in your set texts:

- **Cultural effects:** in what ways does the set text react to its cultural context? What cultural trends affect the style and content of the product?
- **Social context:** how are characters shaped to create representations that are relevant to the historical context of the product?
- **Historical effects:** what big historical events have shaped the product or are reflected within the narratives offered? To what extent is the product reacting to the political landscape in which it is situated?
- **Economic context:** how have economic factors shaped the product? How has the budget of the product shaped its ability to deliver genre-based expectation? How have commercial imperatives shaped the product?
- **Audience saturation effects:** in what ways have audience needs shaped the product? Where do moments of genre subversion create novelty or surprise?

Exemplar: Tide advert (Eduqas). Tide's 1950 advert (see Figure 1.2) conforms, in many senses, to the advertising expectations of the period, using 'Z' line layouts and illustrated imagery to deliver familiarity. Yet the product also tests many of those expectations – using an intertextual reference to wartime propaganda to acknowledge audience nostalgia. This poster's female lead, however, firmly repositions female readers within the domestic sphere – further acknowledging the social changes wrought through wartime demobilisation. Neale would suggest that the poster, in this sense, offers genre-driven familiarity, yet simultaneously tests those expectations as a result of the product's unique social and historical context.

More exemplar analysis and set text help is available for a range of products at www.essentialmediatheory.com

---

Genre hybridity: contemporary media products

Neale suggests that contemporary media products are also marked by their use of genre hybridity – the deliberate inclusion or intertwining of conventions from across a number of genres. Contemporary dramas like *Stranger Things*, for instance, pastiche a number of genre-driven tropes. The otherworldliness of Eleven's experimentation is culled from science fiction, while *Stranger Thing's* creature-based antagonist is a horror borrowing. The potential appeal of genre hybridity to contemporary media makers can be described as follows:

- **Hybridity enables quick tonal shifts:** products can quickly invoke the various emotional intensities of a number of genres through hybridity. Switching from a science fiction setting to the isolation of a conventional horror house, for example, can move an audience from awe to fear within the time frame of two scenes.
- **Genre piggybacking:** products can cash in on the relative popularity of a genre-driven product by incorporating elements or motifs of that genre. The enormous popularity of *The Walking Dead*, for instance, prompted a rush of shows that used zombie-driven motifs.
- **Creates individual product character:** hybridisation allows products to construct originality by mixing ingredients from pre-existing media products.
- **High and low culture remixing:** hybrid products allow producers to shape products that have serious subtexts while also deploying narrative content that is accessible and popular.
- **Expands audience appeal:** combing romance with comedy, for example, expands the target audience of a product to include males and females.
- **Nostalgia:** hybrid products often revive genres, applying nostalgia to satisfy audience sentimentality.
- **Knowing audiences:** contemporary audiences are far more knowledgeable than those of audiences in the past. Hybrid products acknowledge and reward that media knowledge through the use of intertextuality and allusion.
- **Mirrors contemporary audience consumption experiences:** hybridity replicates the multi-channel, media-meshing consumption experiences of contemporary audiences through the simultaneous presentation of disparate genres.

Box 4.3 Think about it: genre hybridity in the contemporary media landscape

- Do contemporary audiences expect their media to be hybridised?
- Which of your set text products provide examples of genre hybridity and for what reasons are those products hybridised?

Concept 2: industry effects on genre-driven content

Auteur-based effects

In creative terms, the writers, stars and directors of products often deflect and subvert genre-driven themes to accommodate the stories they want to tell. The *Star Wars* reboot serves as a classic example of this process: it is, first and foremost, a science fiction product, yet the directorship of J.J. Abrams significantly shaped the story to accommodate his own auteur-driven concerns. Abrams' obsession, for instance, with lens flares and moments of poetic stillness are clearly laid on top of the film's sci-fi driven aesthetic.

Genre planning and institutional mediation

The broader effect of media institutions on genre output is enormous – both in terms of scheduling effects and the impact that a parent media company's values have in shaping genre-driven output. Media schedules, Neale says, are dominated by a number of genre-specific openings. In film marketing, horror films are scheduled for Halloween releases, while family oriented blockbusters are premiered during school holidays. In television, big budget dramas are premiered in autumn to take advantage of the boost to viewership that dark evenings bring. Historical dramas are constructed for Sunday evening broadcasts, while diet shows are commissioned annually to cash in on audiences' New Year health resolutions. In short, media organisations, Neale tells us, effect calendared production routines using genre-driven content as a key planning tool.

Genre-driven content, Neale tells us, is also shaped as a result of producer-oriented practices. The approaches taken by individual television production companies or by the editorial teams of single news titles will invariably subvert genre-based conventions using their own house styles and templates. *The Guardian*, The *Times* and *The Telegraph*, for instance, are all broadsheet newspapers which, broadly speaking, publish the same sorts of content – politics, sports, hard news and so on. Yet the teams of journalists who construct each title are wholly different to one another in terms of their writing styles and political leanings. In this sense the styling and application of genre-driven ingredients work alongside the wider institutional needs and skill bases of the individuals working within those institutions.

The same process is evident in the television industry, the output of which is dominated by a fixed number of genres and subgenres. Crime drama, for example, is a staple ingredient in most UK broadcasters' schedules, with most products deploying victim/perpetrator-driven characters within a police procedural narrative. But again the values of the commissioning broadcaster provide a fundamental steer to the final product. BBC crime dramas will be guided by their public service broadcasting ethos – perhaps foregrounding diversity and new talent as a key ingredient. Conversely, commercial broadcasters might try to garner mass audience appeal through the use of star power and a more mainstream take on genre codes.

Box 4.4 Apply it: diagnose the auteur and institutional effects on genre-driven set texts

Auteur effects

• Who are the key personnel who shaped the set text? Identify writers, directors and performers.

• In what ways have auteurs placed their own personal stamp on the product? What is that stamp?

Institutional effects

• What kind of media organisation commissioned and made the set text?

• How has the organisation type (public service broadcaster, commercial, conglomerate, etc.) shaped the narrative or styling of the product?

• How have budgetary factors influenced the product?

• How has scheduling and distribution shaped the product?

The marketing functions of genre

Neale also alerts us to the use of genre as a marketing tool, outlining the importance of genre within the 'intertextual-relay' (Neale, 2001, 39) of a product (trailers, posters, reviews, etc.). Genre labelling, Neale tells us, is an important feature of marketing – used predominantly to give an indication to audiences of the specific satisfactions that a product will generate. This material, Neale says, inadvertently plays a crucial role in defining the genre of a product for the following two reasons:

• **Intertextual-relay builds a product's narrative image.** Marketing materials determine what Neale calls the 'narrative image' (Neale, 2001, 39) of a product. The genre-based labels used by publicity material and those applied by reviewers and critics fix the genre of a text before it is released. These genre-based stamps can be very hard to shift afterwards.

• **Intertextual-relay guides audience readings.** Publicity builds audience expectation, which, Neale argues, play a huge role in framing audience readings. Audiences, he suggests, adapt their viewing conclusions as a direct result of these labels.

Box 4.5 Apply it: diagnose the use and effect of intertextual-relay on set texts

Locate genre labelling in promotional material

• How is genre foregrounded within publicity material?
• How does imagery, *mise en scène*, costume, colour, setting, etc. construct genre-driven expectations for the target audience?
• In what ways is genre foregrounded within language components of intertextual-relay?
• Is genre labelling visible within reviews, credits, headers or taglines?
• In what ways is genre inferred through star power?

Explain why genre labelling is used

• What narrative pleasures does genre labelling suggest to the audience?

- In what ways does genre labelling help create a recognisable identity for the product?
- Does genre labelling take advantage of cultural trends through piggybacking effects?

Exemplar: *The Jungle Book* **(OCR).** Both the 1967 and 2016 trailers use genre labelling to develop a clear narrative image for both versions of *The Jungle Book*. The 1967 film is advertised as a 'musical high-flying singing adventure', signalling action-based narrative expectations, while also suggesting that the product will afford pleasure through spectacle. The 2016 remake is less overt in its application of genre labelling, yet the foregrounding of adventure-based expectations is constructed by the 'makers of Pirates of the Caribbean' intertitle. Similarly, the trailer's otherworldly setting and minor key soundtrack suggest genre hybridity through the presence of fantasy-based motifs. The application of hybridised intertextual-relay, in this instance, expands the target audience of the product by piggybacking on the success of other genres and the critical acclaim of the *Pirates of the Caribbean* franchise.

Further set text help is available for a range of products for all exam boards at www.essentialmediatheory.com

Table 4.1 Speak Steve Neale

Auteur effects	Relates to the input that individual producers have on genre-driven products.
High/low culture remixing	A common form of genre hybridisation in which products mix pop culture genre forms with motifs from more serious genres.
Hybridisation	Using the styles, narratives or other motifs from multiple genres in one product.
Iconography	The visual components of a media product. Iconography might refer to *mise en scène* elements (settings, costume and acting style) or to other stylistic devices (camera work, editing treatments, layout or typography).
Institutional mediation	The effect of institutions in shaping genre-driven products. Institutions might take a specialised approach to genre production or might shape genre output as a result of their company type/ethos.

Intertextual-relay	Refers to the range of production and marketing materials that are used by products (trailers, posters, reviews, press packs, interviews and so forth). Intertextual-relay fixes the narrative image of a product through genre labelling.
Narrative image	Refers to the set of expectations and persona built for a media product through marketing and the reception of the product by its audience.

Table 4.2 Neale: ten minute revision

Concept 1: *the pleasures afforded through repetition and difference*
- The genre of a product is determined by a variety of factors.
- Genres offer specific pleasures to their audience.
- Audiences enjoy genre subversion as well as repetition.
- Genres are not fixed but are subject to constant change as a result of real world effects and the needs of audiences.
- Genre hybridisation is a common feature within the contemporary media landscape.

Concept 2: *industry effects on genre-driven media*
- Genre-driven output is shaped by auteurs and is also subject to the effects of institutional mediation.
- Genre labelling is widely practised by media producers to create a narrative image for a media product.
- Promotion and marketing materials (intertextual-relay) can fix the genre of a product.

Two theorists who might challenge Steve Neale's thinking
- **Stuart Hall:** would agree that products construct pleasure for audiences, but would also emphasise the potential dangers that certain genres have in effecting audience ideologies through genre specific character representations and stereotypes.
- **James Curran and Jean Seaton:** might challenge the notion that genre hybridisation is not a significant feature of the contemporary landscape. Curran and Seaton suggest that media concentration has in fact led to fewer experimental forms and that media companies are instead overly reliant on tried and tested narrative formulas that are designed to garner mass audience appeal.

5   Postmodernism
Jean Baudrillard

Baudrillard refused to adopt the stiff academic tone used by many of his predecessors and contemporaries in his writing, producing instead an almost prophetic and strident set of texts that feel out of place within wider academia. Yet, the impact of Baudrillard's writing has been enormous, introducing a whole new glossary of media terminology – hyperreality, media implosion and simulacra – to suggest that contemporary mass media messages are inescapable and all-consuming yet, conversely, empty of meaning. As the academic William Merrin tells us, Baudrillard's books are, 'standard reference points for any understanding of our cultural processes' (Merrin, 2005, 5).

Key concept: the real and the hyperreal

Baudrillard's key argument stems from his observation that society has experienced three distinct stages of cultural evolution that he labels 'the precession of simulacra' (see Box 5.1). In many ways, Baudrillard's precession relates the story of twentieth-century secularisation and the replacement of religion as society's primary meaning maker by the mass media. The three phases of Baudrillard's precession can loosely be described as follows:

- **Phase 1 – Early modernity.** This covers the period from the Renaissance to the Industrial Revolution. In this stage, cultural products (literature, music and art) map closely to what Baudrillard calls 'a profound reality' (Baudrillard, 2018, 6). Culture, in this sense, creates an authentic experience when consumed. Mass culture, moreover, is dominated by the lone voice of religion and connects the masses to a singular ideology – to one version of the world. Culture, too, Baudrillard tells us, is 'sacramental' in that it communicates profound spiritual experiences. As a result, early modernity produces authenticity and a collectively agreed set of truths about the world in which we live.

• **Phase 2 – Modernity.** The second phase, modernity, covers the period from the Industrial Revolution to the Second World War. In this stage, religion and religious certainties begin to fragment, eventually giving way to early mass media forms like cinema, radio and photography. During modernity, Baudrillard argues, the authenticity and collective truths of early modernity begin to 'dissimulate' (Baudrillard, 2018, 6), breaking down into competing versions of reality.

• **Phase 3 – Postmodernity.** The final phase, the phase in which we now live, is labelled 'postmodernity'. In postmodernity, Baudrillard argues, mass media forms dominate culture, replacing the single voice of religion with the multi-channel, multi-media whirlwind of contemporary mass media. This, Baudrillard tells us is the age of 'hyperreality' in which cultural products no longer reference the deeper unified significations that religion once provided. In the postmodern era, culture is fragmented, its meanings and instructions are temporary, its messages commercialised and inauthentic.

Box 5.1 Know it: why does Baudrillard describe culture as a 'simulacra'?

Baudrillard uses the word 'simulacra' to suggest that culture (mass media, religion, art, etc.) produce versions of reality to help explain our place and function in the universe. Christian religion, for instance, constructs a version of reality in which, crudely speaking, God is said to have created the universe in seven days. Of course, God did not create the world in seven days. This assertion is an early religious story that attempted to explain the complexities of the universe before science could give us a more accurate picture. Culture, of course, authors numerous other stories that attempt to explain the world we live in. Importantly, Baudrillard argues, these cultural products, or versions of reality, are in fact 'simulations'. The 'precession of the simulacra' refers to the way in which those 'simulations' have changed since the Renaissance.

The ecstasy of communication

Significantly for Baudrillard, the technologies of the mass media have helped construct what he calls an 'ecstasy of communication' (Baudrillard, 1987, 11), arguing that the process of meaning making has exponentially expanded in the postmodern era, permeating modern life in ways that lie far beyond the cultural capacities of previous historical periods. Baudrillard identifies the following effects of postmodernity:

- **The media is everywhere.** In today's hyperreal world, every bus hoarding, street corner and shop window is an advertising opportunity – indeed, our public spaces are so saturated with media that it is almost impossible to avoid the tidal wave of cultural messages beamed at us.
- **Our private spaces have been invaded.** Baudrillard tells us, too, that today's hyperreal media even penetrates the once safe havens of our family homes. There is no escape, Baudrillard says, from the incessant chatter of hyperreality: 'One's private living space,' Baudrillard writes, 'is conceived of as a receiving and operating area, as a monitoring screen endowed with telematic power' (Baudrillard, 1987, 17).
- **Authenticity is impossible to find or keep.** Because the hyperreal world of modern media is so all-encompassing and so incessant, Baudrillard tells us, the deluge of messages offered have limited significance. Cultural products in postmodernity construct throw-away messages, forgotten almost as instantly as they are consumed.
- **Repetition and duplication effects.** The postmodern media, Baudrillard further argues, repeats and repurposes content in a never-ending chain of replication. Commercially successful products are repurposed, remade, serialised or copied to attract and maintain audiences, while genre-oriented storytelling replicates narrative formulas in endless echoes of products that are themselves copies of something that was made a long time ago. In this sense, Baudrillard tells us, we know the end of any news event before it has happened. We know how our box-sets will resolve or how our gaming cut scenes will play out, because 'everything is already dead and resurrected in advance' (Baudrillard, 2018, 6).

Box 5.2 Think about it: what effect does postmodern hyperreality have on audiences?

- To what extent is it true that we live in world in which it is impossible to escape the reach of media? Is it possible to completely escape the reach of the media?
- In what ways have smartphone ownership and the digital revolution expanded the reach of hyperreality?
- How many media products have you seen today? How many advertisements have you seen? How much time have you spent on social media?
- How many media messages have a deeper meaning or connect us to authentic or satisfying experiences?
- Is it true that the contemporary media duplicates and replicates the same stories over and over? Can you provide any examples of this?
- Has media proliferation meant that we have lost touch with the natural world?

Meaning implosion

The proliferation of media comes at a further cost in that the variety of arguments and opinions presented via television, news and online media makes it difficult for audiences to reach an objective conclusion about the real world. News outlets, for instance, produce a version of the world that we implicitly understand to be biased towards one political viewpoint, and in today's media landscape it does not take too long to locate an opposing source or contradictory analysis.

Indeed, products internally neutralise content through the use of opposing opinion editorials or balanced reportage. The resulting effect is to present a world in which simultaneous truths exist – a presentation, moreover, that lacks both objectivity or certainty and that leaves media audiences to effect what Baudrillard calls hyperreal 'inertia' (Baudrillard, 2018, 68), a kind of mesmerised inability to act.

The age of advertising

'Promotion,' Baudrillard writes, 'is the most thick-skinned parasite in our culture. It would undoubtedly survive a nuclear conflict ... it allows us to turn the world and the violence of the world into a consumable substance' (Baudrillard, 2018, 31). Whereas the age of

---

Box 5.3 Apply it: locating 'meaning implosion' in newspaper set texts

- Do your newspaper set texts offer oppositional points of view?
- How might those presentations affect audience readings of those news stories?
- In what ways are audiences immune to the ever-present nature of news media?
- Are audience reactions to news events minimised as a result of the ever-changing cycle of news stories?

Exemplar: *The Daily Mirror* (Eduqas). The multiple perspectives offered across different newspapers and also within single products – as evidenced in *The Daily Mirror* set text through the diverse opinion editorials of Corbyn, Blanchard and Jones – leads to what Baudrillard calls 'meaning implosion'. The ideas and meanings of news products are neutralised, leading audiences to respond with what Baudrillard describes as 'hyperreal inertia' – a mesmerised yet transient engagement that prevents readers and viewers from gaining an objective sense of the real world at large.

Further set text help is available for a range of products for all exam boards at www.essentialmediatheory.com

---

modernity was dominated by cinema and photography, advertising, Baudrillard tells us, presides over the postmodern age. That ascendancy, Baudrillard further explains, has important repercussions in that the narrative strategies laid down by television and print-based advertising form a story blueprint that influences other media products, while also configuring audiences to respond to those narratives with hyperreal 'inertia'.

Advertising, Baudrillard suggests, holds us in a hypnotic state of 'superficial saturation and fascination' (Baudrillard, 2018, 91), teaching us from an early age that the mesmerising ideals of commercial advertising are rarely realised in real life. The ensuing mistrust of commercial media imagery, Baudrillard further argues, is readily applied to other media forms. We are compelled to watch, he says, but we do not quite believe what we see.

Baudrillard suggests, too, that the language and narrative structures of advertising have infected other media products. News bulletins, for

---

Box 5.4 Apply it: how might advertising lead audiences to respond with hyperreal inertia?

Advertising set text applications

• Do your set text advertising products nurture mistrust? Are they too ideal to be believed?

• In what ways do the exaggerated worlds of the advertising set texts feel fake or too ideal?

Exemplar: Maybelline – That Boss Life (AQA). That Boss Life constructs a conventional transformation narrative, aiming to position its audience to think that the use of its Big Shot product will ultimately lead to an idealised metropolitan New York lifestyle. The use of slow motion sequences, of flawless presenters, and of the golden ambience of the product's penthouse setting presents a dream-like tone that is both seductive and mesmerising. Yet, Baudrillard would also argue, audiences intuit that the world depicted lies beyond their reach and that its hyperreal gloss is both inauthentic and fake. Audiences might be seduced, Baudrillard argues, but they are also inert, and, more dangerously, that inertia carries into the readings made of the wider media those audiences consume.

Further set text help is available for a range of products for all exam boards at www.essentialmediatheory.com

---

example, are reduced to easily digestible packages, their stories built upon the same strategies of suspense and revelation that we find in short-form advertising. Politicians, too, Baudrillard argues, have sacrificed debate and argument for news friendly sound bites designed to effect political branding and voter seduction. Drama, too, pulses in shorter and shorter scenes, while YouTube vloggers have swallowed, wholesale, advertising's commercial mantra by commodifying themselves – branding themselves in the same way that a shampoo advert might affect audience appeal via choreographed representations of impossible ideals.

Fictionalised reality / realised fiction

The blending of media forms is a further symptom of our hyperreal age. Baudrillard tells us that products borrow and steal at will in order to attract our attention in today's media saturated landscape. As a result, contemporary media forms have blurred fact and fiction to the extent that, Baudrillard argues, audiences can no longer tell them apart. Documentaries cast their participants as if they were actors, deliberately orchestrating moments of narrative crisis to produce entertainment. *Geordie Shore*, *TOWIE* and *Love Island* might cast participants from the real world, but no one is fooled. Contestants knowingly engineer their onscreen selves to maximise the opportunities such shows present, guided, of course, by the careful hand of TV producers so that their cast might satisfy audience expectation. There is little that is 'real' in today's reality TV.

Baudrillard suggests that the news similarly effects an ever-present discourse of fictionalised crisis, generating daily doses of real life entertainment that are populated by cameos of TV savvy politicians and business leaders who are media trained so that they might deliver news friendly sound bites. News narratives, too, replicate the language and imagery of disaster movies. The news is a never-ending soap opera, packaged into easily digestible parcels, into three act narratives that are instantly forgotten once delivered. Any meanings and emotions produced are temporary, Baudrillard argues, replaced by the next news cycle in an 'accelerated circulation of meaning' (Baudrillard, 2018, 80).

The shallowness of contemporary media hyperreality, Baudrillard further argues, produces a deep yearning by media audiences for products that provide authenticity. The endless churn of contemporary culture, he tells us, produces a requisite desire for stability and validity that the media tries to satisfy through nostalgic appeals and an attempt to embed reality in programming.

The real world has thus become a staple ingredient in postmodern fiction. Biopics and historical drama readily reinterpret history without due regard for historical accuracy – repackaging the world of yesterday using stock characters and audience-friendly narrative formulas. Horror films also call upon their audiences to believe that their narratives are genuine through the ubiquitous 'based on real events' tagline. The word 'based', of course, gives due licence to magnify, distort or change any element of the writer's choosing. And, of course, soap operas, crime dramas, family dramas and work-based dramas purport to offer us a view of the world using the tropes of realism to convince us of their actuality, yet do so in ways that reflect nothing of reality at all.

Box 5.5 Think about it: does the media produce a fictionalised version of reality?

- To what extent are audiences aware that reality TV is manufactured?
- What TV products do you watch that claim to deal with real life yet depict reality using the strategies of fictional products? Think here about documentaries, historical dramas, biopics and even the news.
- What fiction-based narrative strategies do non-fiction forms use to present real world events? Think about characterisation, story structure, editing techniques and language devices.
- Can fictionalised realities have an impact on the real world?

Box 5.6 Apply it: diagnose the use and effect of 'realised fiction' in your set texts

- Do any of your set texts use historical settings as their story premise?
- Do shows make appeals to audience nostalgia?
- Do shows blend archive footage with drama to convince us of their real world settings?

Exemplar: *Deutschland 83* (OCR). Baudrillard suggests that the surface values of postmodern hyperreality produce a deep yearning for that which is authentic or real. Arguably, the use of historical verisimilitude as a narrative ingredient within fictionalised television drama creates products that anchor that need through the use of nostalgia. *Deutschland 83* clearly evidences this approach. The use of authentic footage of 1980s icon Ronald Reagan provides an instant point of nostalgic reference for the product's audience, further reinforced within the title sequence through its archive-driven montage. *Deutschland 83*, however, also references an imagined or fictionalised East Germany – the East Germany of television spy movies. It's canted cinematography, it's spy-based characters (the rebel, the double agent, the master spy) are stereotypical expectations of the genre. The resulting blend of fact and fiction leads us to conclude that *Deutschland 83* is most assuredly a postmodern text – a text that Baudrillard might suggest distances us from authentic experience rather than bringing us closer to it.

Further set text help is available for a range of products for all exam boards at www.essentialmediatheory.com

Table 5.1 Know it: Baudrillard's three phases of the simulacra

Phase	Historical time period	Key features
Early modernity	Renaissance to the early Industrial Revolution	• Limited cultural production. • Cultural production is dominated by a few authors (the church and the state). • The masses are held firmly in their positions by cultural messages.
Modernity	The Industrial Revolution to the Second World War	• Cultural representations begin to break down – producing multiple versions of reality. • Cultural production is dominated by the bourgeoisie and legitimises the capitalist system. • Mass media forms dominate.
Postmodernity	Post Second World War onwards	• The media produces hyperreality – an explosion of meaning. • The media makes everyone a consumer – audiences have a limited relationship with authentic meanings. • Advertising and television ascend as the dominant cultural forces. • Contemporary digital technologies accelerate the effects of postmodernity.

Table 5.2 Speak Jean Baudrillard

Hyperreality	Baudrillard suggests that we are unable to separate the real world from that which is manufactured by the media. In this sense we live in a world that is beyond reality or is hyperreal.
Inertia	The constant stream of media that we are subjected to paralyses us or makes us unable to feel or act in a way that creates deep meaning.
Meaning implosion	The sheer volume of media and the multiplicity of voices within the contemporary media landscape produces a cocktail of opinion and counter opinion that audiences cannot disentangle.
Media blending	Media forms in the postmodern age blur – the narrative strategies of news, for example, become absorbed into fiction and vice versa.

Table 5.3 Baudrillard: ten minute revision

Key concept: *from the real to the hyperreal*
- Baudrillard suggests that there have been three distinct cultural phases: pre-modernity, modernity and postmodernity.
- We now live in the postmodern age which is marked by a massive proliferation in media content and media messages.
- Media proliferation has resulted in an implosion of meaning through the simultaneous presentation of oppositional truths.
- Media proliferation is enabled through the endless copying of pre-existing media. Media forms 'blend' and hybridise during this copying process.
- The postmodern age is marked by the dominance of advertising as a media form. Advertising has also impacted on other media forms creating hyperreal inertia.
- Baudrillard suggests that media blending has resulted in the construction of fictionalised reality.
- Audiences yearn for authenticity in postmodernity; the media industry tries to satisfy this yearning through realised fiction.

Two theorists who might challenge Baudrillard's thinking
- **Roland Barthes:** would argue that media products have a clear relationship with reality. Media texts represent and naturalise the world views of those who hold power in society.
- **Henry Jenkins:** would contest the idea that postmodernity results in hyperreal inertia. Contemporary digital media, he would argue, can make a positive difference in the real world through the use of participatory culture.

6 Representation

Stuart Hall

When we talk about representation effects we are prompting discussion about the way the media makes us think about the world at large: the way, for instance, that the news reconstructs real world events or the processes that television and film adopt to tell us about the world beyond our screens.

Hall's contribution to our understanding of the representational processes used by the media cannot be underestimated. His academic work helped to construct an understanding of how the media industry and the routine production practices employed by the media shape our understanding of the world in subtle and not so subtle ways. Hall, too, shone a critical light on media's ability to manufacture and reinforce social inequalities through stereotyping practices and, more importantly, he articulated an understanding of how those representations might be subverted and resisted.

Concept 1: media representation processes

The 'reflective' school of thought

One view of the media is that television, print and online products reproduce the real world without distortion. According to this view, the media acts like a mirror – capturing and relaying a faithful version of the real world to audiences everywhere. The joy of consuming media, in this sense, is that it can take us to places we have never been to. The media provides a window to the world, a faithful and accurate means of reproducing information that we might ordinarily be unable to access. Accordingly, the job of media professionals – news journalists, documentary film-makers and so on – is to observe and record these inaccessible wonders so that audiences at home can similarly bear witness.

Representations are built via codes

Stuart Hall acknowledges the imitative capacity of the media. The camera, he tells us, reflects the real world around us. If we record or photograph a countryside scene, a version of that scene is created in which the trees, grass and land are accurately depicted. But, Hall reminds us, professional media representations offer us more than just imitation. Media products, he tells us, are composed through the selection and ordering of visual, aural and linguistic elements. Media products, in this sense, do not offer us accurate or objective reflections of the world at large, but rather produce versions of reality that are shaped by the subjective viewpoints of their creators.

A news story, for example, might tell us about a real world event, but the way that story is relayed – through the use of linguistic effects or supporting imagery – produces an edited version of the event reported. News stories are encoded using stylised features – through the deployment of emotive headlines or edited imagery that audiences have learned to decode as a result of their previous exposure to similar imagery. In this sense, the media not only contributes to our understanding of the world, but also uses a shared symbolic language that audiences have internalised through their media experiences.

A portrait image that is photographically composed, for instance, tells us a great deal about the individual depicted – whether that subject is powerful or powerless or, indeed, whether we are meant to like that person at all. A fourth wall break can connote authority. A subject who directs their gaze to the left of the frame might infer regret or nostalgia, while a high angle composition might suggest vulnerability or helplessness. Importantly, Hall tells us, our ability to decode such imagery is not innate – we are not born with an innate knowledge of photographic composition. Our ability to decode the meanings of media imagery, Hall argues, is produced as a result of our continued exposure to media products. The media, therefore, both uses and shapes our shared understanding of the real world around us.

Box 6.1 Apply it: identify representational codes used in your newspaper set texts

News stories create representations of real world events through the careful selection of language, layout and design. These representations can:

- Lead audiences to a predetermined opinion – so, perhaps, they form the same conclusions as those people who make the media.
- Reflect the editorial viewpoint of the paper – offering a politically biased view of real world events.
- Be sensationalised to create reader engagement.

Use the following questions to help you decode the representational effects constructed by the front pages of your set text newspapers:

Language analysis

- Do headlines or copy use emotive language? What connotations do specific words convey?
- Are stories constructed using emotive semantic fields? (A semantic field is a collection of words that are themed – for example, war, gun, enemy, destruction.)
- Does the article use sibilance (repeated 's' sounds), cacophony (harsh or discordant sounds) or euphony (gentle sounding words – usually the letters 'f' or 'l')? What connotations are constructed as a result of these sounds?
- Is the story reported from a specific point of view?
- Who is the reader guided to empathise with in the story?
- Who is the reader guided to blame?
- Are statistics or facts used to create impact?
- What kinds of sources are used to evidence the story and with what impact?

Image use

- Why has the image used been chosen? What story does it tell?
- How does the composition of the image assist in creating a specific effect? Think in terms of eyelines, tilt and camera distance.
- What connotations are suggested through body language, setting, costuming and colour use?
- How is the meaning of the image anchored by accompanying captions or headers? How does this secondary information guide the reader towards a predetermined conclusion?

Layout

- Are keywords emboldened or underlined?
- What colours dominate within the layout and with what connotative effect?
- How does layout suggest the importance of the news event reported?

Concept 2: stereotypes and power

Hall tells us that media products do not just reflect reality; their meanings are shaped by media producers, and, in turn, those versions of reality have a profound influence on audience thinking. In this sense, Hall argues, we can say that media products have a discursive effect – that, in other words, they produce ideological inferences for their readers and viewers.

Hall was particularly interested in the media's portrayal of black masculinity, initially investigating newspaper reportage in the 1970s in which black mugging stories were a staple feature. He concluded that media stereotyping during the period firmly linked black masculinity with criminality and, moreover, that the media's reliance upon such stereotypes had a profound and complex effect on wider social attitudes.

Stereotypes, Hall tells us, are important for the following reasons:

- **Media stereotypes reflect social attitudes.** Hall argues that media stereotypes reflect the wider views of society – by studying the media we can gain a sense of what wider society thinks about those groups that are routinely stereotyped. Hall's work looking at black youth culture identified, for instance, that the stereotypes associating black males with criminality reflected a deep-seated anxiety about real black crime. Journalists who reported black criminality were therefore reacting to the genuine fears of their audiences when writing and publishing these stories.
- **The media contributes to the construction of stereotypes.** Media stereotyping, Hall further argues, significantly shapes social attitudes regarding specific groups. For example, he concluded that black youths internalised the criminal stereotypes constructed by the media in the 1970s and, as a result, engaged in real criminal

activities. The demonisation of black youths by newspapers also meant that white audiences were reluctant to trust young black males, significantly hampering their employment prospects and further channelling young black men to engage in criminal activities to survive.

•   **Stereotypes can be reshaped or repurposed.** Hall also identifies that media stereotypes can be guided towards positive representations of key groups. Indeed, the changing nature of black representation within the news since the 1970s is testament to the idea that media stereotyping processes are highly fluid.

The essentialising, reductionist and naturalising effect of stereotypes

Hall suggests that stereotypes are incredibly powerful and that their widespread use guides audiences to associate specific groups with negative traits. Stereotypes, moreover, infer a symbolic social power, helping to position some groups as social outcasts or, as Hall suggests,

---

Box 6.2 Know it: why are stereotypes used by the media?

Stereotypes are universally deployed by the media for the following reasons:

•   **To help audiences to understand characters.** Using stereotypes provides a visual shortcut that enables audiences to instantly decode a character through their use of body language, costume, etc.
•   **To help audiences build character relatability.** Stereotypes build audience empathy, sympathy or antipathy very quickly.
•   **To signpost audiences.** Stereotypes help audiences gain a sense of the potential direction of a story – we understand that certain events will happen to certain characters: princesses will fall in love, the dumb blonde dies first in a horror movie, the action hero will probably triumph in spite of the adversity faced.
•   **To reinforce genre expectations.** All genres contain stock characters – indeed an audience's enjoyment of a given genre might be driven by those characters.

as social 'others' (Hall *et al.*, 2013, 215). Stereotyping is thus a form of symbolic violence for Hall – an efficient means to hold socially undesirable groups at bay without using actual physical action. Stereotypes, Hall argues, are an unusually effective means of social control because:

1 **They increase the visibility of key groups:** stereotypes usually depict groups by referencing a few key negative features – behaviours, physical appearance, etc. This highlights the undesirability or 'otherness' (Hall *et al.*, 2013, 215) of those groups and enables that sense of 'otherness' to be efficiently communicated to the rest of society.

2 **They infer that negative traits are natural:** the few key ingredients used to construct stereotypes are repeated so often by the media that those ingredients are interpreted by audiences to be fixed or natural qualities. So stereotypes infer that black males are *naturally* lawless or that dumb blondes will *always* lack intelligence.

Hall argued that stereotypes accordingly construct 'closure and exclusion' (Hall *et al.*, 2013, 248) – fixing the boundaries of what or who is socially acceptable, while excluding all other groups from that elite list. Criminalising stereotypes, for instance, exclude black males from the normal workings of society. And because social exclusion produces limited access to economic or cultural power, stereotyped groups find that they cannot fight the representations that are constructed on their behalf. This self-reinforcing process leads Hall to conclude that media stereotyping creates power 'circularity' (Hall *et al.*, 2013, 251): those groups with economic or cultural power get to create stereotypes, while the impact of those stereotypes makes it impossible for powerless groups to escape from their lowly social positions.

Box 6.3 Research it: identify common negative stereotypes used by the media

Work with your classmates to research how the following groups are represented by the media – use your own knowledge to supplement the list of areas suggested for study.

Ability-based stereotypes
Possible areas to investigate: groups with physical disabilities, representations based on mental health.

Age-based stereotypes
Possible areas to investigate: teen girls, teen boys, teen subcultures, representations of the elderly.

Class/region-based stereotypes
Possible areas to investigate: chavs, single mothers, northerners, southerners, working class representations.

Ethnic stereotype
Possible areas to investigate: black males, black women, Asian men, Asian women, Muslim groups.

Gender-based stereotypes
Possible areas to investigate: dumb blondes, the bitch boss, the nerd, fathers, mothers.

LGBTQ stereotypes
Possible areas to investigate: gay men, butch gays, lesbian stereotypes, transgender representations.

For each of the six clusters above:

- Identify the visual cues, costume codes and behaviours that are used by the media to construct the stereotypes within each group.
- Identify media products that contain examples of the stereotypes listed above.
- Create a collage for each of the groups above to help you identify the visual cues used to construct stereotypes.
- What ideas do stereotypes naturalise about the groups they represent?
- Which social groups are immune to media stereotyping?

Challenge question

- In what ways do the stereotypes uncovered help to maintain the economic powerlessness of the groups they represent?

Visit essentialmediatheory.com to explore the stereotypes listed above in more detail.

Box 6.4 Apply it: what are the effects of the stereotypes used in your set texts?

Identify stereotypes constructed of marginalised groups

- What stereotypes do your set texts create?
- What behaviours or physical traits are used to identify those stereotypes?
- What ideas about these groups are naturalised as a result of the use of stereotypes?
- How do the stereotypes used reinforce existing power structures or help to exclude key groups from mainstream society?

Diagnose the 'internalising' effect of stereotypes

- How might set texts lead marginalised groups/individuals to internalise attitudes or beliefs that are problematic?
- What particular moments in the set texts might lead to internalisation?

Challenge question

- In what ways might we apply Hall's idea of 'power circularity' to give further weight to arguments regarding the potentially negative impacts of media stereotyping?

Exemplar: *Humans* (Eduqas). Despite Channel 4's public service broadcasting oriented commitment to promote media diversity, we can clearly see that *Humans* uses stereotyped characters that Stuart Hall would highlight as problematic. Non-white characters are excluded from power in the show – for example, the robot prostitutes working alongside Niska are mostly black, while the Turkish gangster responsible for selling black market synth technology is depicted using an ethnically-oriented criminal stereotype. Of course, these characters are invoked to create instant visual cues for the audience and, while these moments might reflect wider social inequalities, they also exclude these groups

from hegemonic power. Hall points, too, to the potential for stereotyped behaviours (in this case, black prostitution and Turkish
criminality) to be internalised by audiences in a way that reinforces
those behaviours as ethnically appropriate social norms. Exclusion of
those groups as 'others' by a white audience might also lead, Hall tells
us, to their economic exclusion in the real world.

Further set text help is available for a range of products for all exam boards at
www.essentialmediatheory.com

Transcoding and stereotypes

Despite the difficulties faced by socially excluded groups in combat-
ing negative stereotypes, Hall tells us that cultural representations
are not fixed. The process of representation, he infers, can be
thought of as a battleground with each articulation of a stereotype
reaffirming or reseeding the suggestions of that stereotype. Representations can and do change as a result, their meanings slide or
transform. Stereotypes, moreover, can be contested and their meanings subverted.

Hall also argues that media producers who want to challenge pre-
existing negative stereotypes generally have to graft new meanings
onto those existing presentations. He calls this process 'transcoding'
and outlines three important strategies that makers can deploy to shift
negative stereotypes:

1   **Appropriated representations:** by commandeering negative
    stereotypes, their meaning, Hall argues, can be devalued or sub-
    verted from within. Grime musicians, for instance, have purpose-
    fully appropriated the hyper-masculine stereotypes associated with
    black masculinity – repurposing this negative stereotype as iconic
    or powerful for black male audiences.
2   **Counter typical representations:** this process combats neg-
    ative connotations by producing representations that reverse
    stereotypes. Butch gay representations, for instance, invert tradi-
    tional gay representations of male homosexuality as weak or
    passive.
3   **Deconstructed representations:** stereotype contestation can be
    achieved by narratives that explain or lay bare the effects of stereo-
    typing. Deconstructed stereotypes add contextual information that

Box 6.5 Apply it: locate moments of transcoding in your set texts

Use the following questions to help you locate moments of transcoding in your set texts and to diagnose their effect on audiences:

- Do any of your set texts appropriate stereotypes? Where is appropriation most visible and what effect might its use have on the product's audience?
- Which products deploy countertypes? What stereotypical attributes are reversed by the countertype? What assumptions are challenged through the use of countertypes?
- Which products explore stereotypes through deconstructions? Which moments in the text could you use to provide the examiner with relevant analysis?

Exemplar: Adbusters, Christian Louboutin Spoof advert (Eduqas). Adbusters contests mainstream ideologies through the use of deconstructed transcoding (Stuart Hall). The Louboutin parody, in many senses, conforms to conventional mainstream representations in its depiction of black Africa as poverty stricken. Yet the juxtaposition of that stereotype against symbols of first world privilege moves the reader beyond a simple analysis of black Africa as 'other' to white Europe – indeed, the superiority of those Western values is implicated as the cause of African poverty and immediately undercuts the standardised meanings of the stereotype used.

Further set text help is available for a range of products for all exam boards at www.essentialmediatheory.com

helps audiences to forge a deeper understanding of the experiences of the group being stereotyped. In *I, Daniel Blake*, for instance, class-based stereotypes are relayed in the form of the single mothers, Geordies and chav-based representations. The film, however, humanises those characters through emotive backstory.

Table 6.1 Speak Stuart Hall

Closure and exclusion	Media products exclude groups from power through representation – often positioning marginalised groups as unworthy of social inclusion.
Internalisation	Internalisation occurs when marginalised groups or individuals assimilate the behaviours of negative media representations.
Naturalisation	The repeated messages of stereotypes can suggest that groups have a natural disposition towards certain types of behaviour.
Other	Hall suggest that those groups who are excluded from social power or mainstream culture are 'others'.
Power circularity	Stereotypes both reflect social attitudes and simultaneously reinforce them through processes such as internalisation.
Symbolic violence	Stereotypes that demonise groups offer us moments of symbolic violence in that they lead to the exclusion of those groups from social power.
Transcoding	Refers to representation strategies that contest stereotypical assumptions.

Table 6.2 Stuart Hall: ten minute revision

Concept 1: *media representation processes*
- The media does not mirror real world events but produces an edited version of the events depicted.
- Media representations are constructed through codes – through the use of language, imagery, layout, sound and editing.
- The media plays a vital role in shaping our views of the wider world.

Concept 2: *stereotypes and power*
- Stereotypes are used by media producers to create instant characterisation.
- Stereotypes reduce social groups to a few key traits or visual cues and suggest that those groups are naturally inclined towards a specific set of negative behaviours.
- Stereotypes are mostly found where there are huge social inequalities. They exclude and demonise groups in a manner that both reflects and reinforces social hierarchies.
- Social groups can internalise the behaviours inferred by stereotypes.
- Stereotypes can be contested through transcoding strategies.

Two theorists who might challenge Hall's thinking
- **Stuart Hall:** Strangely, Hall himself provides a substantial challenge to his own ideas. His reception theory model suggests that audiences can resist the effects of the media through the production of oppositional or negotiated readings.
- **Paul Gilroy:** In many senses, Gilroy's work picks up on many of the themes of Hall's arguments – his analysis, however, suggests that racial stereotypes are framed by the wider cultural/historical forces of Empire. This makes it much harder for the media to contest black stereotypes because they are so deeply entrenched within the British cultural psyche.

7 Postcolonial theory
Paul Gilroy

Like Hall, Gilroy explores the construction of racial 'otherness' as an underlying presence within print media reportage during the 1970s and 1980s, arguing that criminalised representations of black males regularly stigmatised the black community.

By the 1990s, however, Gilroy shifts his attention to consider the mass media constructions of British identity in postindustrial Britain. He subsequently diagnoses the existence of a media induced 'postcolonial melancholia' as a representational response to the UK's declining global position in the late 1990s. That decline, Gilroy tells us, is realised as a result of the loss of the post-war Empire – a loss that the media cushions with stories that are infused with Union Jack waving nostalgia. For Gilroy, problematically, those stories are also underscored by racial misrepresentations and the amplification of multicultural disharmony in the UK.

Concept 1: racial binaries, otherness and civilisationism

Racial otherness

Gilroy's hugely important study of black representation, *There Ain't No Black in the Union Jack*, traces the story of UK race relations from the Second World War onwards, in which the post-war wave of immigration from the West Indies produced a series of anxieties regarding immigrant behaviour. He draws attention to, 'Lurid newspaper reports of black pimps living off the immoral earnings of white women' (Gilroy, 2008, 95) and suggests that the public's association of these post-war immigrants with substandard living conditions produced racial representations that were 'fixed in a matrix between the imagery of squalor and that of sordid sexuality' (Gilroy, 2008, 97). Such representations, Gilroy argues, marginalised the immigrant black community from the outset – constructing them as a racial 'other' in the predominantly white world of 1950s Britain.

In the two decades following the Second World War, media stories regarding the black community, Gilroy suggests, intensified fears that immigrant communities might swamp white Britain. Those fears were further concentrated in the late 1970s and the 1980s through news coverage that routinely associated the black community with assaults, muggings and other forms of violent crime. 'It is not then a matter of how many blacks there are,' Gilroy writes of the period, 'but [of] the type of danger they represent to the nation' (Gilroy, 2008, 105). Blackness and criminality, Gilroy argues, thus became a 'common sense' feature of the media.

During the 1970s and 1980s, newspapers also related stories concerning the many community riots of the period, often depicting these multi-ethnic disturbances as black only events, and further suggesting the black community was naturally prone to lawlessness and incompatible with white British values. The Notting Hill Carnival riot of 1976 serves as a particularly poignant example, with the rioters described by various newspapers as 'an angry army of black youths' and 'as coloured men in screaming groups' (Gilroy, 2008, 122). The anxieties, Gilroy argues, surrounding individual acts of black criminality – muggings, assaults and so on – tilted towards more generalised descriptions of black criminality, while the political concerns of the black community regarding heavy-handed policing tactics were largely ignored.

Gilroy, too, points to a number articles that inferred black culture's corrosive effects on white youth during this period. For instance, in 1982 *The Daily Mail* reported the detention of several Eton pupils on drugs charges, suggesting that the boys' descent into criminality was prompted by Rastafarian influences. For Gilroy, the story is emblematic of the kinds of racial binaries that the media constructed during the period in which the traditions of white civility – in this case Eton – were increasingly subject to the corrupting influence of a black 'other'.

Civilisationism

For Gilroy, the 9/11 World Trade Centre terrorist attack in 2001, and its aftermath, radically altered both the tone and nature of media-oriented

Box 7.1 Think about it: representations of 'otherness' in the contemporary media

We can sum up Gilroy's main points as follows:

* Second World War immigrants were seen as an alien 'other' to an imagined white Britishness.
* Black immigrants were perceived to be 'swamping' white communities.
* Black communities were demonised through representations that associated them with individual acts of criminality – knife crime and muggings were particular media concerns. These representations construct a 'common sense' notion of the criminal black male.
* Later representations constructed the black community in general, and black youths in particular, to be naturally lawless and incompatible with British white values.
* Later representations suggested that black otherness had a corrosive effect on white youth culture too.

Are the representational anxieties outlined above constructed by the British media today?

* Do contemporary media products continue to produce stories that revolve around 'swamping' themes?
* Are some communities constructed as 'other' by the media? Who and how?
* Are some communities associated with criminal behaviours?
* Are some communities constructed as having a corrupting influence?
* What evidence could we use to suggest that the media has moved on from the kinds of representations of the black community that were created during the 1970s and 1980s?

representations regarding race and racial difference. The Anglo-American response to the attack is perhaps best summed up by then US President George W. Bush's 2002 State of the Union Address in which he declared that North Korea, Iran and Iraq constituted, 'an axis of evil, arming to threaten the peace of the world' (Bush, 2002). For Gilroy, Bush's speech consolidates a deeply troubling and imperialist view of global politics that justified foreign intervention on the grounds that Western democracies were morally superior to all other nations. Gilroy's further disquiet

Box 7.2 Apply it: do your set texts construct a civilisationist subtext?

Media depictions that construct stark contrasts between Western readers and Islamic fundamentalism can be located in news and TV drama. Use the following questions to assess the effect of set texts that deploy representations of this nature:

- How do the representations nurture audience fear?
- How do representations dehumanise extremist subjects?
- What effect do these representations have in constructing racial hierarchies?
- Do any of your set texts deconstruct civilisationist assumptions?

Exemplar: *The Daily Mail* and *The Sun* front pages, Monday 18 February 2019 (all exam boards). 'Civilisationist' representations, Paul Gilroy argues, are notable for their stark worldview, often presenting a simplistic binary opposition in which Muslim fundamentalism battles Western democratic ideals. The front covers of both *The Daily Mail* and *The Sun* often confirm this civilisationist perspective – the reportage surrounding the pregnant 'Jihadi Bride' Shamima Begum, for instance, and her application to return to the UK after joining Islamic State of Iraq and Syria (ISIS) terrorists is, Gilroy would suggest, deeply problematic. Within that reportage, *The Daily Mail* constructs a sense of Muslim incompatibility, foregrounding the girl's lack of repentance and unwillingness to reintegrate into UK culture while also outlining the existence of 'dozens' of other girls in similar situations. *The Daily Mail* further exaggerates the 'swarming' potential of the story by telling us that the UK might be 'forced' to repatriate the girls. *The Sun* (see Figure 7.1) also infers an overriding lack of public sympathy, while the accompanying photo of black clad hijab-wearing women nursing Shamima's baby constructs a deliberately unsettling depiction of Muslim motherhood. Both papers create an exaggerated sense of fear, using the Muslim 'other' to source that danger.

Further set text help is available for a range of products for all exam boards at www.essentialmediatheory.com

Figure 7.1 The Sun front page (Monday 18 February 2019).

© Sun/News Licensing.

surrounding 9/11 is that the media readily accepted and repeated Bush's 'axis of evil' worldview. Gilroy collectively labels these post 9/11 representations as 'civilisationism'. Civilisationism, he argues:

- **Constructs a binary worldview:** President George W. Bush famously declared 'Either you are with us, or you are with the terrorists'. Civilisationist depictions construct similarly stark worldviews, positioning media audiences to internalise a simplistic binary that divides the globe into the opposing forces of fundamentalist terrorists and a morally superior West.

- **Has a racist subtext:** For Gilroy, the 'war on terror' rhetoric of the post 9/11 era perpetuates a long-standing racial hierarchy in which Muslim subjects are positioned as inferior.

- **Nurtures cultural incompatibility:** Because the media is so focused on global conflicts and terrorist action, an inference is made that European and Muslim groups are incompatible communities. Yet, Gilroy reminds us, that generalised inference of racial incompatibility is a media fabrication. Real world racial integration, or 'cosmopolitan conviviality' (Gilroy, 2004, 9) as he calls it, is wholly different. Indeed, racially diverse communities live with few, if any, day-to-day effects of racial difference.

- **Nurtures fear:** For Gilroy, the political repercussions of civilisationism have enabled the construction of a 'securitocracy' (Williams, 2013, 44) – the use of repressive measures by Western democracies that are designed to keep nation states terrorist free. In this way, the inhuman treatment of prisoners in Guantanamo Bay, for example, or the torture of terrorist subjects are justified as necessary measures.

Concept 2: the legacy of Empire and British identity

In his 2004 book, *After Empire*, Gilroy suggests that we live in 'morbid culture of a once-imperial nation that has not been able to accept its inevitable loss of prestige' (Gilroy, 2004, 117). The British, he argues, are undergoing a crisis of national identity: the loss of the British Empire, further compounded by the devolution of Northern Ireland, Scotland and Wales, has forced a collective question regarding British identification. 'Is Britain's culture now Morris dancing or line dancing?,' Gilroy asks, 'Are we Gosford Park, Finsbury Park or the park and ride?' (Gilroy, 2004, 130).

The loss of British colonial prestige and the resulting contraction of the UK's global influence have largely been airbrushed from public discourse, Gilroy argues, yet that contraction in national importance has simultaneously affected a deep-rooted cultural anxiety accompanied by a sense of national rootlessness and guilt. For Gilroy, moreover, the immigrant population has become an outward symbol that perpetually reminds the UK nation of its loss of global power. Empire immigrants and their descendants, he argues, are a visible representation of British power as it once was. Post-war racism, he further suggests, also acts as a covert attempt to recover and purify the social order – to restore the English nation to its pre-war state.

The immigrant, Gilroy argues, is also a symbol of British exploitation and of the racial violence perpetuated in the name of Empire, reminding us that colonial expansion and the British imperial project gave birth to the British slave trade and to the brutal repression of indigenous populations across the colonies. The Empire, as such, represents more than the loss of sovereign power. It is also a stain on the collective British identity, the ramifications and extent of which have never been fully explored or acknowledged by the nation as a whole.

World War victories and Albionic Englishness

Gilroy tells us that the twin pull of Empire guilt and the loss of British global power have resulted in a national postcolonial melancholia – a sort of collective depression that both absorbs and blinkers the British outlook. The media, Gilroy suggests, compensates for this collective depression by routinely invoking the mythic victories of the Second World War to distract the national populous from its loss. Indeed, Gilroy reminds us that numerous other British military campaigns and over 70 years of history have elapsed since 1945, yet the Second World War remains a potent media symbol that is routinely invoked by the British media.

The Second World War, Gilroy argues, acts as a powerful set of signifiers that enables us to turn the loss of the British Empire into a moment of significant historical and ideological victory. As such, the media routinely conjures up the spirit of the blitz and the bulldog mentality of Winston Churchill to remind us of our once important historical significance. The media's mythologising of the Second World War, Gilroy further argues, revels in the isolation of Britain and the preservation of an imagined English purity. Wartime allusions, as a result, are routinely invoked in sports and news reportage, with a nostalgic English nationalism adopted as the standard response to World Cup fixtures, Olympic coverage and European politics. Gilroy, too, draws attention to the media's preoccupation with British tradition as a further response to postcolonial melancholia. The news' obsession with the Royal family and television's routine depictions of the quintessential English rural landscape invoke, Gilroy suggests, an inward looking Albionic Englishness. The media manufactures a long-lost imagined England untouched by the demise of Empire – an England, more importantly, in which racial diversity and multicultural conviviality are strangely absent. Albionic England is the film world of Bridget Jones; it is the English summers that abound in advertising, The Proms and Royal weddings. It is also the English rurality of historical drama – of ITV's *Victoria* and of Netflix's *Crown*. Albion, too, is traceable in *Emmerdale*, *Midsomer Murders* and *George Gently*. But, Gilroy warns, Albion England is nothing more than a distracting fantasy that disguises the reality of what Britain is really like – crippled by regional poverty and an ever-widening economic social divide.

Box 7.3 Discuss it: to what extent are we infected by postcolonial melancholia?

- Is the British media obsessed with the past? Are we a backward-looking nation that cannot come to terms with our diminishing global role? What evidence from the media could you present to support or contradict this idea?
- Why are British newspapers so obsessed with the Royal Family? Do they represent order in a chaotic modern world? Do they represent British tradition?
- Does the media construct an Albionic representation of Britain – a largely white, rural version of England that is celebratory? What products have you seen that construct this imagined version of England?
- Why do you think the media constructs these idealised representations of Albion?

Box 7.4 Apply it: diagnosing postcolonial melancholia in your set texts

Search for moments that affirm Gilroy's view that the UK has been paralysed by postcolonial melancholy. Use the following to help you construct relevant analyses:

- Do any of your set texts create an Albionic representation of the UK? Do they foreground an idealistic or traditional view of England?
- Do the set texts use traditional English institutions to assert an Albionic view? Are they overly concerned with the Royal Family? Do they invoke a traditionally Christian representation of England? Do the set texts defer to English tradition in an idealised way?
- Do the set texts invoke nostalgia or, more specifically, war-oriented nostalgia?
- Are the set texts used to explore/search for an English identity? Do the texts foreground identity anxiety?
- Do the set texts use immigrants as a means of prompting Empire guilt?
- Do the set texts explore hostile attitudes towards immigration?

Exemplar: *The Guardian* online, 19 February 2019 (OCR). *The Guardian* exemplifies much of Gilroy's assertion that the UK media exudes postcolonial melancholia. Its online home page is rich with stories that exemplify English anxiety – the paper's lifestyle section, for example, routinely offers identity advice for an audience struggling, in Gilroy's view at least, to navigate the postcolonial landscape. Articles variously ask burnt-out readers whether they 'Should embrace the power of no?' or ask 'Google: would my life be happier without it?'. *The Guardian* also exemplifies Gilroy's identification of postcolonial Empire guilt. The newspaper's commission of the *Black Sheep* documentary, for instance, charts the experiences of contemporary Nigerian second-generation immigrants against the distinctly non-Albionic backdrop of underclass Essex. White racism is accordingly portrayed as an endemic feature of British society by the short film, the reader is positioned, in Gilroy's view, to witness the melancholic spectacle of a disintegrating Britain.

Further set text help is available for a range of products for all exam boards at www.essentialmediatheory.com

Table 7.1 Speak Paul Gilroy

Albionic nostalgia	A representation of Englishness that is marked by nostalgia and generally produces a whitewashed version of an idealised/imagined rural England.
Civilisationism	A stark representation of the world in which Western democracy is pitted against extremist others.
Cosmopolitan conviviality	A term that describes real world multiculturalism and the high levels of racial harmony that mark most people's day-to-day existence. Conversely, the media portrays racial disharmony as the norm.
Postcolonial melancholia	A term used by Gilroy to describe the deep-rooted shame felt as a result of the loss of the British Empire. That loss is deflected through media nostalgia and a widespread anxiety surrounding British identity.

Table 7.2 Gilroy: ten minute revision

Concept 1: *racial binaries, otherness and civilisationism*
* Black communities are constructed as an 'other' to white culture and are associated with criminal activity and lawlessness.
* The media reflect civilisationist attitudes through simplistic reportage and the demonisation of Muslims – media products nurture fear and the idea that Muslims and Europeans are incompatible.

Concept 2: *the enduring legacy of the British Empire on English identity*
* A deep-seated postcolonial melancholia infects the media as a result of Britain's diminishing global importance.
* Postcolonial melancholia prompts a nostalgic construction of Englishness.
* Postcolonial melancholy produces a sense of English rootlessness and an anxiety surrounding British identity.

Two theorists who might challenge Gilroy's thinking
* **David Gauntlett:** would present a far more optimistic picture of the media's capacity to effect change or to enable positive identity construction. He would suggest that the variety of media representations available to contemporary audiences is far greater than that outlined by Gilroy.
* **Henry Jenkins:** would present a far more optimistic view regarding the current media landscape than Gilroy's postcolonial assessment – suggesting that new technologies enable audiences to engage in participatory culture and to form online communities.

8 Feminist theory

Liesbet van Zoonen

Central to van Zoonen's feminist concerns is the idea that culture – art, film, literature, the media, etc. – plays a crucial role in informing audiences, both past and present, of the gender-based roles that they ought to assume. Her concern in investigating contemporary culture is to isolate the processes that have allowed patriarchal ideals to become the dominant ideological force that shapes gender expectations today – a force, van Zoonen argues, that has resulted in the widespread subjugation of women across society.

Concept 1: the female body as spectacle

'A core element of western patriarchal culture,' van Zoonen writes, 'is the display of woman as spectacle to be looked at, [and] subjected to the gaze of the (male) audience' (van Zoonen, 1994, 87). Using Laura Mulvey's psychoanalytic feminist readings of Hollywood, van Zoonen argues that the dominant representation of femininity in Western media is one that objectifies womanhood. From TV game shows to consumerist advertising, from fashion photography to television drama, the sexualised portrayal of women has had, van Zoonen tells us, a powerful and profound effect on male and female understandings of our gendered identities. The widespread practice of objectifying women, she argues, degrades and dehumanises females, while giving male viewers, for whom women are sexualised, an unspoken exploitative power that spills into real world relations.

Objectified representations are formed as a result of a range of highly specific creative practices, including:

- **Male gaze invites.** Female sex appeal is traditionally inferred through direct appeals to viewers using fourth wall breaks. Often those appeals are softened by head tilts or other submissive gestures to create a female passivity. Use of the male gaze also extends to products that have a predominantly female audience (female lifestyle magazines, female-oriented advertising, etc.) – thus suggesting the extent to which female subordination might be internalised by female consumers.

- **Restricting females to secondary roles.** Women are consistently led or controlled by a stronger male presence in media texts. On television they play romantic interest characters or assume supporting roles, while in magazines women are consistently positioned to pursue male-based dependence through advice and relationship-oriented content.

- **Constructing women as passive participants.** Onscreen, females are saved, they do not do the saving. Sports coverage in magazines and news, too, predominantly focuses on male performance, while advertising narratives traditionally position males in more active domestic roles such as DIY or gardening.

- **Framing women differently.** The powerlessness of women in the media is constructed through cinematic tilt downs, low eyeline compositions or soft-focus framing, while costume and make-up conventions further sexualise female media inclusion.

- **Reinforcing narrow beauty ideals.** Western beauty ideals further restrict female participation in the media to a limited number of roles. Women tend to be excluded beyond a certain age or conform to tightly controlled conventions governing physical beauty.

The female spectator

van Zoonen acknowledges the potential power of female objectification, but also questions the idea that women simply adopt a masculine view of femininity as a result of media consumption and argues that a variety of audience effects might result:

- **Female identification.** van Zoonen suggests that female spectators might internalise traditional gender stereotypes that are acted out on screen and that women might come to regard media

beauty myths – the narrow definitions of ideal womanhood presented to us by the media – as something to aspire to.
• **Reading against the grain.** van Zoonen also suggests that the objectification of women by the media does not necessarily lead all women to internalise the male gaze. Audiences, she tells us, 'are no longer ... subjected to the vicious intentions of patriarchal power and ideology, but are considered to be active producers of meaning'(van Zoonen, 1994, 149).
• **Female genres.** van Zoonen, too, acknowledges the huge diversity of texts, some of which produce narratives, character types or representations that fall outside of the usual patriarchal mould. She

---

Box 8.3 Apply it: detecting female objectification in your set texts

Use the following questions to help you construct exam ready analysis that examines the scope and impact of female objectification in your set texts.

• Do the texts limit the roles that women play?
• Are women active or passive in the set texts?
• Do the texts objectify women through composition, costuming or acting decisions?

Exemplar: *Homeland* (OCR). van Zoonen suggests that media-based female representations are problematic in the way they objectify women. Despite its female lead, *Homeland* certainly delivers a range of questionable moments in the set text episode – mostly via the presentation of Brody's wife, Jessica. Her introduction to the audience via an explicit sex scene exists, arguably, to provide erotic pleasure for a male audience. Moreover, the choice of actresses playing lead female roles quietly reinforces the narrow beauty myths of Western culture. The text suggests that female worth is defined through the provision of erotic pleasures, and that those pleasures can only be achieved if women conform to a narrowly defined set of attributes based on age or physique. The impact of these moments, van Zoonen might argue, is that audiences, both male and female, internalise these representational subtexts and, in so doing, perpetuate real world female oppression.

Further set text help is available for a range of products for all exam boards at www.essentialmediatheory.com

draws particular attention to the theoretical work of research that has sought to examine female media forms such as soap operas and romances – acknowledging that these texts might provoke alternative readership patterns that challenge patriarchy.

Economic context

van Zoonen also argues that a clear gender imbalance exists in terms of media-oriented production opportunities, with women often sidelined to administrative rather than technical or creative roles. Some pockets of the media are staffed more prominently by women but, van Zoonen argues, even these are symptomatic of wider social gender inequalities. Radio production, for instance, provides an interesting exception to the male dominated nature of the industry, but only as a result of its perceived secondary status within the sector.

Similarly, media forms that deal with issues that are connected to traditionally female roles – motherhood or domesticity – tend to be made by women. As a result, children's television, educational programming and consumer journalism tend to be made by female practitioners, while more serious media output – news, political journalism and drama – are dominated by male media makers.

Certainly, if we look at the television-orientated set texts identified by the exam boards in 2018, we can clearly see that women were

---

Box 8.4 Research it: who made your set texts?

Research the people who made your set texts and answer the following questions to help you identify the impact of those production teams on the representations created.

Television, music video and radio: who managed the production? Identify writers, directors and producers.

News and magazines: what genders are the journalists who wrote the stories in your set texts? Who are the more senior managers of the set text? Identify editors-in-chief, news editors, section editors and so on, if you can.

- Is there a noticeable gender imbalance in terms of who made your set text products?
- What are the potential effects of that imbalance on story content?

almost totally absent from the senior creative teams that constructed the episodes identified for study. Only one lead writer, Anna Winger, was represented, while only 2 of the 18 texts were directed by female personnel.

Political context: second and third wave feminism

van Zoonen's writing can also be considered to be emblematic of a wider range of feminist activities that took place during the 1970s and 1980s – a disparate movement of thinkers, academics and social commentators that have been collectively labelled the feminist 'second wave'. While the feminist 'first wave' fought for the female vote in the early 1900s, second wave feminism paved the way for equal employment legislation, educational opportunities and cultural empowerment. In highlighting the patriarchal undertones of media objectification and production practice, van Zoonen was similarly hopeful that the media would open up more opportunities for female subversion and female cultural empowerment.

However, the political fervour of the feminist second wave gave way to a generation of female commentators in the late 1990s who viewed the radicalism of their predecessors as too prescriptive. The resulting 'third wave' of feminism advocated a softer feminist agenda, arguing that women themselves were best placed to choose whether they wanted to pursue traditionally female roles or seek career-orientated goals. Third wave feminism, sometimes dubbed 'girlie' feminism, suggested, too, that women could be both mothers and managers, and that the decision to objectify oneself, to use one's body for the purpose of the male gaze, was an individual choice.

Third wave feminism gathered momentum in the 1990s – the Spice Girls gave us 'girl power' whilst Destiny's Child told their female fans that they could both be '*Independent Women*' and beautiful. Third wave female representations have subsequently become a staple feature of the media, compelling the media landscape to include more powerful female representations, while also tempering those representations with values, ideals and outlooks that are traditionally feminine.

The feminist fourth wave

There is considerable evidence to suggest that the more radical agenda of second wave feminism is making a comeback, with audiences using social media, primarily, to voice their criticisms regarding media objectification and to agitate for wider social change. The #MeToo movement, for example, responded to the Harvey Weinstein sex abuse

---

Box 8.5 Apply it: third wave feminism or radical feminism?

It is, perhaps, too simplistic to suggest that contemporary media is wholly saturated with objectified versions of femininity. Use the following questions to help you diagnose which of your set texts challenge traditional gender representations:

- Which of your set texts construct third or fourth wave oriented representations of women? In what ways do these representations construct more positive versions of womanhood?
- How do cinematography, *mise en scène*, lighting or other media language features sustain these positive representations?
- Are representations fostered by female media talent? Who are these influential female creatives?

Exemplar: *The Killing* (AQA and OCR). van Zoonen would suggest that traditional crime drama invokes female powerlessness. The lone wolf male detective, female-oriented victims and objectified support characters are staple features of the genre that reinforce, in van Zoonen's terms, traditional active/passive male/female binaries. Third wave depictions of women, however, have tilted the media landscape towards the creation of more complex female characters, and perhaps provide a more satisfactory description of the representational effects produced by *The Killing*. Sarah Lund is a complex female character, who maintains a traditionally-leaning female role through her family-oriented depiction, while also negotiating a career-oriented role. Her jumper clad, middle-aged characterisation, moreover, provides a further contrast to the conventional objectification strategies of the crime genre and, in doing so, produces a much needed example of gender diversity within television fiction.

Further set text help is available for a range of products for all exam boards at www.essentialmediatheory.com

---

allegations – with women from across the globe using Twitter to share real world experiences of male abuse. Similarly, the online Everyday Sexism Project invites women around the globe to catalogue their experiences of sexism and to call out inappropriate behaviour. In the media, too, there is some evidence to suggest that fourth wave feminism is radicalising female representation. Mainstream music stars like Beyoncé are articulating increasingly politicised pop personas, while TV dramas and sitcoms are giving space to a whole new generation of female writers such as Phoebe Waller Bridge (*Fleabag* and *Killing Eve*) and Lisa McGee (*Derry Girls, Indian Summer* and *Being Human*) – both of whom have been universally applauded for their uncompromising female characters.

Concept 2: masculinity in the media

van Zoonen tells us that the patriarchal ideologies of Christianity banished the male form to the margins of culture. 'From the Renaissance onwards,' van Zoonen writes, 'the representation of the male nude body became exceptional, always causing uproar and prohibitions' (van Zoonen, 1994, 98). Within patriarchal societies, masculinity is constructed to be the socially dominant gender and, as a result, is more likely to be constructed as an active participant within media texts. Moreover, to allow the male form to be subject to a female gaze is censored or controlled because, van Zoonen suggests, the act of looking castrates power. In short, to look or to gaze, she argues, is to assume a position of power. To be looked at suggests, conversely, passivity and weakness.

The dominance of men within society thus leads the media to produce radically different presentations of males than it does of females. Of course, van Zoonen acknowledges the presence of sexualised male imagery in the media, and that some of those images objectify the male body, but she also argues that the male form in contemporary Western culture is, by and large, depicted in ways that allow the male subject to retain authority over the spectator. van Zoonen highlights the following features and processes associated with male representation within the media:

* **The male body is predominantly celebrated through sports imagery.** Sports photography produces representations of masculinity that are designed to connote strength and power, emphasising

movement and skill to reinforce a sense of male dominance over the reader. Perfume adverts, male fashion and so on thus draw upon sports personalities to model products – thus allowing male spectatorship to proceed without erotic objectification.

• **Male eroticisation is romanticised.** Male objectification for female audiences exists, van Zoonen tells us, but is rarely expressed in mainstream forms. When such imagery is produced, moreover, the subversive threat of male eroticisation is often limited by contextualising the imagery within a romantic as opposed to a sexual setting. In women's lifestyle magazines, for instance, men are described in terms of their potential as relationship partners rather than as objects of sexual consumption.

• **The active gaze.** van Zoonen argues that male subjects rarely construct invitational poses. The male gaze, if directed at the viewer at all, is framed by harder body language, offering confrontation or strength rather than passivity. Masculine depictions, too, avoid objectification by directing the subject's gaze to the edge of the frame, or directing it upwards in a show of spiritual strength.

• **Strength not weakness.** van Zoonen also draws attention to the ways in which masculine ideals in media imagery are associated with bodily strength. 'The male pin-up's lack of passivity is one of his important features,' she writes, while 'various signs of activity' (van Zoonen, 1994, 101) are encoded into male imagery to further neutralise any potential for eroticisation.

Box 8.6 Apply it: are masculine ideals constructed by your set texts?

Use the following questions to construct exam ready analysis that considers the impact of masculine representations created by set texts.

• How are the male characters within your television, video game and music based set texts constructed? Do they conform to van Zoonen's assertion that males are normally encoded as active?

• In what ways do *mise en scène*, composition and lighting sustain the representational effects of set texts?

• How significant is sports-related imagery of males in newspaper/ magazine set texts?

• Do any of your set texts construct a subversive version of masculinity? How?

Exemplar: *Life on Mars* (Eduqas). Both Sam Tyler and Gene Hunt reinforce van Zoonen's conclusions regarding the active presentation of masculinity by the media. Sam's high-octane car chase during the introduction to episode one clearly positions him as a conventional action hero from the very start. Similarly, Hunt's no-nonsense hard man persona provides male audiences with an outmoded representation of masculinity in which unrestrained action, male authority and violent power can be subtly celebrated. van Zoonen would suggest these portrayals help to encode real world male power and further reinforce patriarchal ideals as the dominant ideological force within Western culture.

Further set text help is available for a range of products for all exam boards at www.essentialmediatheory.com

Table 8.1 Speak Liesbet van Zoonen

Active/passive representations	Media products, van Zoonen would suggest, encode women to be passive and males to be active within media imagery. Depictions that construct gender in this way reinforce male social dominance.
Male gaze	A stylised depiction of women that invites viewers to take erotic pleasure while viewing the female form. The female gaze is constructed through invitational poses and passive body language.
Objectification	An image that demeans or degrades its subject.
Patriarchy	A society constructed according to a male point of view which, as a result, allows males to become the dominant gender.
Subversive representation	A media representation that challenges or undermines an idea or set of ideas that are widely held within society.

Table 8.2 van Zoonen: ten minute revision

Concept 1: *the female body as spectacle*
- The roles that females are expected to play within society vary enormously across different cultures and historical periods.
- The dominant representational mode in Western culture positions women as an erotic spectacle.
- Second wave feminists have challenged the dominance of men in society.
- Third wave feminists have reasserted the right of women to occupy traditional female roles.
- Fourth wave feminists continue to challenge male privilege using both mass media and social media forms.

Concept 2: *masculinity in the media*
- Masculine depictions are not subject to the same objectification processes as females.
- Male social dominance is reinforced using active representations of masculinity.

Two theorists who challenge van Zoonen's thinking
- **David Gauntlett:** would argue that contemporary media products, both online and mass media oriented, offer audiences a much wider diversity of gender-based identities than is suggested by van Zoonen. This enables audiences to shape their own identities and to resist the ideological pull of patriarchy.
- **Judith Butler:** would agree with much of van Zoonen's thinking, but would suggest further that the use of gender-based labels like 'male' and 'female' mask the complex nature of sexuality. She would also argue that individuals have resisted those conventional labels by engaging in 'gender trouble'.

---

9   Intersectionality
bell hooks

hooks draws attention to the universal silence of commentators and academics alike regarding the black female experience. She contextualises that silence against the wider backdrop of cultural change in America, prompting some awkward questions as to how and why black femininity has been so readily sidelined.

The black civil rights movement of the 1960s paved the way for male black equality, but, for hooks, neglected to explore the experience of ordinary black women. Similarly, the feminist movement of the 1960s gave women – white women – the power to strive for gender equality in the workplace and across society, but again the black female experience was left undiscussed. hooks, in response, places black femininity centre stage, seeking in the first instance to explain why black women were so readily silenced during these two crucial emancipatory moments, while also offering up an emancipatory call to action to communities of all colours and genders across the globe: a political plea to women and men of all ethnicities and nationalities to realise that oppression, in all its forms, is driven by a set of historically entrenched social and cultural conditions.

Concept 1: interconnected oppression

The legacy of slavery

hooks' passionate and highly emotive analysis of the airbrushing of the black female experience is rooted in a historical evaluation of black femininity within the American slave system. Moreover, contemporary black female representations – the oversexed black female stereotype and the black 'mammy' – are the indirect result of the horrific abuse enacted on black women by their white slave masters.

Rape and sexual abuse were a routine feature of female slave life on the plantations in America, with girls as young as 13 years old subject to endemic sexual violence. Sadistic floggings were delivered for any number of minor misdemeanours: for not working hard enough, for burning breakfast or, more disturbingly, if those black slave women and girls tried to resist the sexual advances of their white overseers. Black slave women, hooks tells us, were regarded as little more than a physical commodity used, she further explains, to breed slave children and expand the unpaid workforces who maintained the American plantations.

Significantly, hooks argues, the mistreatment of black women was also sanctioned or encouraged by the wives of plantation owners. The sexual violence perpetrated on black slaves was ignored because it often deflected unwanted attention away from plantation wives themselves. The religious ideals of the white plantation wives, too, fostered sexual purity as a beauty ideal, and meant that the black women who toiled bare breasted in their cotton fields were easily disregarded as unchristian and heathen. Black females were, accordingly, considered to be fallen versions of womanhood, naturally over-sexed, and, as such, considered complicit or culpable when plantation husbands raped them.

The contemporary black female experience

And so begins a cultural process that associates black femininity with overly sexualised stereotypes. Black women, when they do appear in cultural products, often feature as prostitutes or repulsive characters who prey upon weak white masculinity. 'One has only to look at American television,' hooks writes, '...to learn the way in which black women are perceived in American society – the predominant image is that of the "fallen" woman, the whore, the slut, the prostitute' (hooks, 1982, 52).

Perversely, the nineteenth-century white abolitionists who campaigned to end slavery echoed the same sentiment. The abused position of black women was well known, but their experiences were quietly sidelined as a result of the middle class abolitionists' reluctance to discuss sexual abuse in public. Moreover, hooks suggests, the hierarchical position of black women within the slave system and their subservience to all others (including the white wives of plantation owners) made them a less worthy cause. Much of that plantation-based social structure persists today, hooks argues, with white males ascending to economic, social and political positions of power, while beneath them, white females, then black males and finally black women fight for the scraps.

White feminism as covertly/overtly racist

Black women, hooks tells us, sought to escape their lowly social positions and the widespread stigma of oversexualisation by constructing outlooks that mirrored the feminised conservative ideals of their white counterparts. In the 1950s, Black women, accordingly, embraced motherhood and domesticity and were subsequently reluctant, hooks tells us, to join the white-dominated feminist movement of the 1960s and 1970s because they had so embraced these conservative female ideals.

hooks further argues that white feminism itself was equally complicit in omitting black women from women's liberation politics. The suffrage movements of the 1920s, for example, reflected white supremacist ideologies by openly refusing to admit black women as suffrage members; feminist writers in the 1960s and 1970s similarly sidelined the female black experience, jettisoning racial concerns because they were considered too controversial and might derail any emancipatory progress that could be negotiated with white male power brokers. Thus, while white feminism might have suggested that it was advancing the cause of all women, in reality those writers who preached equality knew nothing, nor did they attempt to discover anything, about the experiences of black American women.

Absent representations

hooks suggests that the legacy of black female cultural subordination has resulted in their wholesale absence from mainstream media. Magazine beauty ideals, in the main, are constructed to be white, while in television, advertising and drama, she argues, the few tokenistic black representations that are allowed to break through are dominated by male actors. As a result, black masculinity, she suggests, has come to represent the black community as a whole.

That domination is reflected even today, with the 2018 University of California, Los Angeles (UCLA) diversity report providing concrete evidence of the continued marginalisation of black female roles in American television. Only 85 black male actors, UCLA claim, assumed lead roles in US scripted shows broadcast during 2016/2017. Conversely, 469 lead roles were played by white males and 319 by white women. The number of black female leads was just 56 (UCLA, 2018).

Box 9.1 Apply it: absent black femininity in your set texts

Set texts that lack female black representation can be linked to bell hooks' ideas very quickly. Use these questions to help you diagnose the effects of those absences:

• Which of your set texts contain no representations of black femininity?
• Does that absence suggest that black women are excluded or marginalised? Does that absence reinforce the 'otherness' of black femininity?
• Are black females excluded at the expense of black male counterparts?
• Does the exclusion of black women symbolise their lack of power?

Exemplar: 'Kiss of the Vampire' (Eduqas). This poster articulates the dominance of white masculinity over white femininity via layout and proxemics. Both white females are figuratively subordinated by the lead male, submitting themselves to his active male pose. The total absence, moreover, of any black representations in the poster is interesting in that it mirrors the marginalisation of black women within post Second World War society. bell hooks argues that this invisibility allows white femininity to represent ideal beauty, constructed in this instance by the virginal purity of the two porcelain-skinned models.

Further set text help is available for a range of products for all exam boards at www.essentialmediatheory.com

---

Negative black female stereotypes

The historical mistreatment of black women has also informed a range of media stereotypes of black femininity. hooks outlines the following representations that persist in contemporary cultural products:

• **Jezebels.** Over-sexualised representations of black femininity have significantly shaped perceptions of black women since slavery. They remain common in hip-hop music in which black women are consistently served up as a sexualised side-dressing for black male artists. The widescale presence of the Jezebel in black music, moreover, leads hooks to argue that this stereotype has been internalised by black women themselves.

- **Aunt Jemimas.** Black women have always been associated with domestic service – their role as house slaves on the plantations and their subsequent restriction to domestic roles in America during the 1950s has helped build the black mammy stereotype. Aunt Jemimas are overweight and asexual representations of black femininity, often depicted as maids or servants who loyally serve their white employers without complaint.
- **Sapphires.** The sapphire stereotype is a comedic depiction of black women and is a common staple of talk shows and reality TV. Sapphires usually appear as angry mothers who cannot control their emotions and vilify black women who have power or who do not conform to the passivity of the mammy stereotype.

Box 9.2 Apply it: analyse set texts in terms of their potential use of black female stereotypes

Some set texts might inadvertently offer the stereotypes highlighted above. Use the following questions to help you locate examples and analysis that you can use in your exam.

- What effect does the stereotype have on black or white audiences?
- Is the stereotype constructed as a result of an internalised black identity?
- Is the stereotype typical of the genre in which it appears?
- How does the stereotype contrast with other representations constructed by texts made by the same or similar producers?

Exemplar: *Formation*, Beyoncé (Eduqas). Beyoncé's career is founded, many would argue, on her willingness to use the black female Jezebel stereotype. The performances offered within much of her work is, in bell hooks' view, highly symptomatic of the disempowering over-sexualised female roles that have been constructed for black women throughout our recent cultural history. *Formation* repeats much of the Jezebel formula, in which corseted troupes of women parade their bodies in sexually explicit dance sequences, inviting audiences to view black women as sexually available and highly promiscuous.

Further set text help is available for a range of products for all exam boards at www.essentialmediatheory.com

---

Concept 2: hooks' call to action

Intersectionality as a political and cultural tool

'To me,' hooks writes,

> feminism is not simply a struggle to end male chauvinism ... it is a commitment to eradicating the ideology of domination that permeates Western culture on various levels – sex, race, and class, to name a few – and a commitment to reorganising U.S. society so that the self-development of people can take precedence over imperialism, economic expansion and material desires.
>
> (hooks, 1982, 194)

hooks' concerns are historically and analytically informed, but to pigeonhole her as an ivory tower academic solely concerned with the history of black female representation misses much of the political thrust of her writing. Indeed, hooks' analysis views all forms of oppression – sexism, racism and class-based subjugation – as symptomatic of the middle-class, white male dominated world we live in. The subjugation of these oppressed groups, she tells us, is interconnected. Indeed, the intersectionalist thinkers who have followed hooks' lead have similarly argued that homophobia, transphobia and disability-based oppressions are also brought about as a result white male oppression.

It is also important to understand that hooks' intersectionalist thinking is not just a tool for analysing or describing the world in which we live. Yes, intersectionality points accusingly to problematic media representations, but it is also a political tool – a cultural instrument that

---

Box 9.3 Discuss it: has intersectional thinking gone mainstream?

- In what ways has racism become a mainstream issue? In what ways have contemporary media producers focused more attention on the black female experience in recent years?
- What other movements or media products can you name that have tried to shed light on the abuse of power by white males?
- What evidence is there to suggest that white hegemony is still the dominant force in society?

seeks to nurture products that actively challenge the many forms of oppression that white male patriarchy produces. In this sense, we can describe some products as 'intersectional media' in that they are knowingly designed to draw attention to the effects of white male power. Intersectional media is constructed to:

* **Explore the interlocking nature of oppression.** Intersectional products explore the connections that exist between different forms of oppression, expressing, for instance, how racism and sexism share the same cause or have similar effects.
* **Highlight white male privilege.** Intersectionality seeks to critique the mechanisms that reinforce white male hegemony.
* **Outline economic oppression.** An increasing number of intersectional media products draw attention to the huge wealth gap that exists between privileged white groups and the rest of society; moreover, they draw attention to the privileges that economic power generates for those groups.

Box 9.4 Know it: #BlackLivesMatter – intersectionality in action

The Black Lives Matter (BLM) movement formed in response to the acquittal of George Zimmerman after he fatally shot Trayvon Martin, an unarmed black 17-year-old youth; Zimmerman wrongly thought Martin was about to commit a criminal offence. The verdict compounded accusations that the American justice system was institutionally racist. The twitter hashtag #BlackLivesMatter subsequently served as a rallying call for state-wide protests following Zimmerman's trial, helping BLM to become a global movement.

Importantly, BLM is deliberately shaped by intersectionalist values in that it exists to provides a space for black women and black trans women to express their political voice. Yet the aims of the BLM movement are not simply limited to agitating on behalf of the black female/queer community. 'We work vigorously for freedom and justice for Black people,' BLM writes, 'and, by extension, all people' (Black Lives Matter, 2019). The BLM movement and intersectionalist thinking has undoubtedly shaped the cultural output of the media industry over the last five years, having found support from a host of global megastars including Beyoncé and Jay Z.

- **Give a voice to invisible social groups.** Intersectional media fills in the gaps that absent representations create – telling the stories and giving weight to the experiences of groups who are 'other' to white male patriarchy.
- **Celebrate otherness.** Intersectional media seeks to construct positive as well as critical effects.

Box 9.5 Apply it: diagnose set texts that deliberately provide intersectionalist commentary

Set texts across the exam boards incorporate intersectionalist viewpoints. Locating those texts and finding moments that articulate those views can help you gain premium marks in representation, institution or audience-based questions. Use the following to help you produce relevant analysis:

- In what ways do set texts provide a space to celebrate marginalised identities?
- In what ways do set texts draw attention to social or economic inequalities experienced by marginalised groups?
- In what ways do set texts suggest that those inequalities are shared across different social groups?
- In what ways do set texts call out white male privilege?

Exemplar 1: Massive Attack, *Unfinished Sympathy* (OCR). Massive Attack's one take docu realist music video provides a bell hooks infused intersectionalist critique of American race and class wealth inequalities. The background cast articulates a diversity of participants: whites with disabilities, Latino women, black fathers, mixed ethnic partnerships – all fronted by the accusatory fourth wall break of an unusual black female lead. The effect is to produce a unifying portrait of American wealth inequality, while a conspicuous lack of white male privilege in the video points to a controlling 'other' in this text. Despite the video's underlying critique, the text also provides a celebration of the various groups featured – the golden lighting provides optimism, while moments of tenderness are juxtaposed with the poverty of the streets in a bid to convince the reader of the worthiness of collective action in the face of the economic and social oppression outlined.

Exemplar 2: Beyoncé, *Formation* (Eduqas). Beyoncé might provide us with a number of moments that reflect a white power affirming jezebel stereotype, yet the context of further imagery suggests that those representations are deliberately ironic. *Formation* knowingly references the #BlackLivesMatter movement through the 'stop shooting us' graffiti reference towards the end of the product. The text not only draws attention to the economic disparities and institutionalised racism of America but provides a stream of high key, tilt up images of a diverse range of black female, black queer and black male identities. The text provokes an intersectionalist ideology – simultaneously critiquing the legacy of black slavery while also celebrating those identities that mainstream American culture marginalises, and, in doing so, asks an active audience to question the overly sexualised imagery at the start of the video. In this sense the video affirms bell hooks' intersectional political intentions by calling out the effects of white male privilege.

Further set text help is available for a range of products for all exam boards at www.essentialmediatheory.com

Table 9.1 Speak bell hooks

Intersectional media	Media products that deliberately include or allude to an intersectional viewpoint.
Intersectionality	The exploration of oppression (sexism, racism, homophobia) as having an interconnected or underlying set of causes.
Otherness	hooks suggests that those who are not white or male are 'others' and, as such, are subject to the various oppressive practices of white masculinity.

Table 9.2 hooks: ten minute revision

Concept 1: *interconnected oppression*
- Representations of black women (and men) have been shaped by historical forces.
- Feminist movements of the twentieth century have largely been dominated by a white viewpoint.
- A social hierarchy exists that places white men at the top followed by white women, male ethnic minorities and, last, female ethnic minorities.
- Oppression of minority groups (racism, sexism, ableism, homophobia) are constructs of a white male dominated social hierarchy.
- The lack of black female power results in absent representations and a range of negative stereotypes that some black women have internalised.

Concept 2: *from evaluation to action, bell hooks' call to action*
- hooks' intersectional work does not just provide us with an analytical tool, but also prompts media producers to fashion their products in ways that draw attention to social inequality.
- Intersectional media foregrounds the interconnected nature of inequality.
- Intersectional media celebrates social diversity and gives voice to social groups that have been marginalised by white male power.

Two theorists who might challenge hooks' thinking
- **Paul Gilroy:** would not necessarily challenge hooks, but his work provides a more UK specific framework for evaluating the representation of black people. His analysis highlights the legacy effects of Empire on our notions of ethnicity and national identity.
- **Henry Jenkins:** again, he would not challenge hooks directly, but would suggest that contemporary media products, through participatory culture, can circumvent established media power. Indeed, the online activism of #BlackLivesMatter provides a brilliant example of the power of participatory culture.

---

10 Gender as performance

Judith Butler

Butler's theoretical work is concerned with unearthing the processes, both cultural and psychological, that shape our identities. She is guided, in many senses, by a quest to test orthodox explanations of gender, principally those of the theoretical heavyweights – Claude Lévi-Strauss, Sigmund Freud and Jacques Lacan. Butler's critique of these thinkers is concerned, to a large degree, with the various explanations they give to describe the development of gendered identities that do not fit into orthodox heterosexual categories.

Butler concludes that masculinity and femininity are not naturally given states, but instead are maintained by individuals through everyday acts. Our gendered identities, she argues, are not established at birth, nor are they formed in childhood or adolescence, but are instead realised through a continuous performance of gendered behaviour. The media, more importantly, plays a vital role in providing us with a set of gender-based templates that we use to inform those performances. Moreover, the dominance of heterosexual-oriented representations across media forms, Butler further argues, helps to maintain traditional male and female identities as a social norm.

Concept 1: gendered identities are constructed through repetition and ritual

Butler draws attention to Lévi-Strauss's anthropological work regarding the cultural myths that deal with incest and sex-based taboos. She highlights his conclusions that myths are powerful makers of meaning, both reflecting and defining the way we relate to others in the wider world. Lévi-Strauss suggests that myths tend to reinforce male power as the norm because males are the more naturally dominant gender. Similarly, the absence of homosexuality within mythic stories provides evidence that our natural sexual inclinations are heterosexually oriented.

Butler is also interested in the work of the influential psychologist, Jacques Lacan, who, she tells us, similarly defines male and female genders using a binary straightjacket. The word 'binary' infers that there are only two possible gender states – male or female – and that normal male/female relations are heterosexually inclined. Lacan argues, furthermore, that our gendered identities are fixed when we emerge from infancy and identify our independence from the world around us. The discovery of the phallus by boys during this transition, Lacan suggests, prompts a symbolic awakening – a moment when males realise they effect sexual power. That awakening, he further argues, translates into masculine social power. Female infants, conversely, are defined through the symbolic discovery that they are phallus free, and the real-isation that they are castrated and socially powerless.

To Lacan, and perhaps comically to us, the realisation of having, or not having, a penis naturally creates the patriarchal social structures in which we live. Importantly, for Butler at least, Lacan further defines homosexuality as an aberration of those symbolic awakenings or as becoming established as a result of heterosexual disappointment during formative sexual encounters.

Butler also examines the work of Sigmund Freud, who similarly explains same-sex affection as a form of melancholia, formed by boys through an unnatural rejection of the mother during the Oedipal phase, or, for girls, as an over-identification with the mother figure during the Electra stage (see Box 10.1 for further explanation). Freud suggests that these key moments in infancy inform lifelong behaviours and, moreover, that homosexuality produces a mental aberration as a result: a kind of depressive melancholia that forms as a result of the realisation by gay individuals that conventional heterosexual satisfac-tions will not ever be realised.

Butler's gender revolution

Butler offers a complex and devastating critique of these three corner-stones of twentieth-century thinking. Her principle objections run as follows:

- **Male and female identities are not naturally configured.**
  Butler's critique of Lévi-Strauss points to the array of gender-based

identities that exist in addition to heterosexuality. Butler tells us that these non-heterosexual identities, and the relationships that non-binary individuals form, are built on desires that are just as valid as those experienced by heterosexuals. Their exclusion from myths and other cultural products reflects, Butler infers, the wider marginalisation of these groups in society.

* **Gender does not exist inside the body.** Butler critiques the notion that gender – whatever it is – is stored within the body as if it were something akin to a soul. Freud's assertion that our sexual identities are internalised during the Oedipal phase is illusory – our gendered identities, Butler argues, are realised through our desires, sexual contacts and physical expressions of love. Our gendered identities are not a fixed object; they are constituted as a result of our behaviours.

* **Gender is not solely determined by primary experiences during childhood.** For Butler, the Lacanian of Freudian idea that our gendered identities are fixed during infancy is a myth that serves to reinforce a heterosexual ideal: a socially imposed ideal. Our genders, Butler argues, are far less stable than Freud or Lacan suggest in that we continuously form and reform our sexual identities throughout our lives.

Box 10.1 Help box: what is the Oedipus/Electra complex?

Freud argued that children become very aware of their genitalia at the age of three – this stage leads to the development of intense emotional attraction to the parent of the opposite sex and to feelings of jealousy towards the parent of their own sex. Boys (through the Oedipus complex) fall in love with their mothers and hate their fathers, while girls (the Electra complex) become attached to their fathers and develop intense jealousy of their mothers.

For boys, the intense rivalry for their mother's affection leads to an internalised fear that their fathers will castrate them as punishment. Boys, Freud suggests, have to reposition their fathers as role models to avoid being emasculated, and in copying their father's masculine behaviour they assume a male identity. Girls, conversely, will eventually realign their love for their mothers (thus creating their female identity) but will also retain their love for father figures.

Box 10.2 Discuss it: what are the problems with the arguments used by Lévi-Strauss, Lacan and Freud to explain how we construct our gendered identities?

Claude Lévi-Strauss

- What criticisms could be made of the idea that our genders are fixed by nature? What other factors might contribute to the creation of our sexualities or gender-based notions?
- If our genders are not naturally fixed, why do so many cultural stories construct heterosexuality as the norm? Can you identify any myths or fairy tales in which homosexuality even features?

Jacques Lacan

- Does the discovery of a penis really invest men with a sense of internal power?
- Lacan argues that homosexual desires form as a result of heterosexual disappointment – does this theory describe a natural process? Is this idea formed, perhaps, as a result of his own heterosexual vantage point?

Sigmund Freud

- Can we really explain adult same-sex sexual attraction as the result of rejecting or over-identifying with our parents at a very early age?
- In what ways is Freud's description of homosexuality as 'melancholic' problematic?

Butler's alternative gender model

Butler puts forward an alternative view of our gendered identities that can be summed up as follows:

- **Our genders are culturally rather than naturally formed.**
Butler tells us that our biological anatomies do not determine our genders. The normalisation of heterosexuality is established, she further argues, as a result of long-standing social rituals that orientate us towards traditional male and female roles.

- **Our genders are not stable but are constructed through repeated actions.** Rituals and performative actions constantly reinforce our identities: the act of wearing make-up, for instance, or dressing in female or male clothing fosters an illusion that we have a seamless and permanent male or female identity. Similarly, our mannerisms and behaviours work as learned micro-performances that continuously signal our identity to ourselves and to others. Importantly, those gender-based cues can be learned or imitated from media products.

Concept 2: gender subversion and gendered hierarchies

Butler might argue that our identities are an open story, but she also acknowledges that heterosexuality is the dominant identity mode in our culture. To maintain an identity that falls outside of the hetero-sexual norm in our society is, she suggests, a subversive act that takes a great deal of effort to maintain. Subversion is difficult Butler argues, painful even, because heteronormative ideals are so deeply entrenched within the fabric of language and other cultural practices.

Box 10.3 Challenge it: challenging heteronormativity is painful

Butler argues that it is incredibly difficult or painful to assume a non-heteronormative identity. Media narratives mirror this assertion, often constructing gay characters who have to seek acceptance from friends and family or who have to confront homophobic intolerance.

- Can you name any media products that use storylines that reinforce the idea that gender subversion is difficult?
- To what extent are those storylines outmoded?
- Can you think of any media products that offer us more positive representations of non-heteronormativity?
- In what ways do the target audiences of products affect non-heteronormative representations?

Gender subjugation

Butler argues that non-heterosexual identities – male homosexuality, lesbianism, transgender identifications – are socially suppressed in favour of heteronormativity. Heteronormativity privileges traditional male and female identities while also promoting heterosexuality as a default relationship model. The subjugation of identities that fall outside of conventional heteronormativity, Butler tells us, can be effected through physical coercion: gay men, for instance, can be compelled to attend conversion therapy by concerned family members or punitive physical deterrents can be deployed to prohibit same-sex relationships (Somalia and Sudan, for example, apply the death penalty as a deterrent for homosexuality).

More importantly, heteronormativity and male patriarchy are reinforced through cultural practices that position non-heterosexuality and female empowerment as a social taboo. Butler draws our attention to the following media processes that commonly marginalise female power and non-heteronormativity:

- **Absent representation.** The sheer lack of alternative representations in the media helps reinforce heteronormativity/male power as the norm. Analysis by the Gay and Lesbian Alliance Against Defamation (GLAAD) found that, in 2018, only 8.8 per cent of American prime time television shows regularly broadcast non-heterosexual characters – a figure that represents a significant increase on the previous year, but still establishes heterosexuality as the ideal social model. Absent representation allows straight relationships to take centre stage as a behavioural norm, while relegating other media representations to the margins of broadcasting. GLAAD, interestingly, identified Netflix as industry leaders in terms of lesbian, gay, bisexual, transgender and queer (LGBTQ) representations in 2018, with 88 non-heteronormative characters used across its programming (GLAAD, 2019).
- **Abjected representations**. Butler acknowledges the theoretical work of Julia Kristeva (see Box 10.4) in suggesting that heterosexuality and male power are reinforced through the suggestion that alternatives to those identities are disturbing, repellent or unnatural. Narratives, for instance, that focus on sex change operations create physical abjection of trans people through the presentation of graphic surgical procedures. Depictions that focus on castration and so on have a deeply unsettling effect.

• **Parodic representations.** Media presentations of homosexuality often use exaggerated masculine or feminine behaviours in a comedic way, through, for instance, overly camp presentations of gay men. Parodic characterisations of this nature produce questionable humour while also reinforcing the idea that homosexuality is an aberration. Yet, for Butler, parodic representations also create what she calls 'gender trouble' and draw audience attention to the performative nature of gender per se. The drag queen, for example, who represents anatomical masculinity yet performs a traditionally feminine role reveals to the audience a sense that all our identities might similarly be constructed or, in Butler's words, that 'the inner truth of gender is a fabrication' (Butler, 2007, 186).

Box 10.4 Help box: Julia Kristeva and female abjection in film

Film theorist Julia Kristeva famously argued that horror films rely on a range of well-worn strategies that repulse audiences through the use of female-oriented depictions that are intended to be disturbing or unsettling. Films like *Carrie* or *Teeth*, for example, create their horror effects by referencing and distorting female bodily functions (menstruation, birth or female sexuality). For Kristeva, the cultural effect of such depictions is to reinforce the idea that the female body is somehow taboo or needs to be hidden from public view, which, as a result, consolidates patriarchal power.

Box 10.5 Discuss it: how does the media present gender subversion?

Absent representations analysis

• How many of your set texts contain prominent LGBTQ representations?
• Why do you think that LGBTQ representations are missing from media products?
• Why do you think Netflix leads the field in terms of including characters that are gender diverse? Could this be related to the target audience of Netflix?

Hierarchical subjugations

- Can you think of any mainstream products, including your set texts, that have constructed problematic LGBTQ representations? In what ways are these portrayals negative?
- Can you think of any products that deliver abjectified LGBTQ representations?
- Can you think of any products that construct comedic or parodic characters who are non-heteronormative?

Box 10.6 Apply it: using Judith Butler to explore representation effects in set texts

Use the following questions to help you find moments in your set texts that can be explained or interpreted using Butler's ideas:

Concept 1: gender as performance

- Are there moments in the text in which characters openly perform a gender-based identity?
- Do the set texts give advice to their audience on how they might perform their genders?
- How do magazine set texts help their readers/viewers adopt traditional male or female roles?
- Do the set texts provide alternative models of gender or sexuality?

Concept 2: reinforcing hierarchical binarisms

- Are the set texts dominated by heteronormative representations? Are lead characters presented within conventional family units? Do lead characters follow heteronormative love interests?
- Does the set text give space to marginalised or non-binary identities? How much space is given to these moments? What is the effect of any absent representations?
- Do the set texts present marginalised identities in a way that creates abjection?
- Do the set texts offer moments that subvert traditional heteronormative expectations? Are these moments constructed as painful or difficult? In what way do those representations reinforce hierarchical binarisms?

Exemplar 1: Zoella (Eduqas). Zoella's YouTube output centres around the production of make-up tutorials and haul-based videos. In a Butlerian sense, Zoella is providing her 12 million subscribers with a pattern of ritualised gender performance via this content – evidencing, in a very literal sense, the means through which she, and they, can assume an orthodox female identity. The controlled application of make-up and the careful selection of fashion wear provide a gender performance template that audiences can use to reinforce their own feminine identities. It is interesting to note that in one particular upload, 'Zoella Does My Make Up', Alfie Deyes becomes the gender-troubled subject of that feminine transition. The result, Butler would argue, simultaneously offers male and female viewers a drag version of Alfie that is both comic (and hence abjecting), while also constructing the liberating/unsettling possibility that masculinity per se is a performance-oriented construct that can be easily manipulated.

Exemplar 2: *Teen Vogue* (AQA). *Teen Vogue* presents itself as 'the young person's guide to conquering...the world'. It certainly contains articles that are designed to raise political awareness, but much of its online content is dedicated to giving fashion and beauty advice to its young female readership, and, Judith Butler might argue, this advice provides young women with the rituals and performative templates needed to assume a socially acceptable female identity. 'Do try these at home', the webzine suggests, enabling *Teen Vogue's* audience to perform a version of socially sanctioned femininity through the hair and make-up routines presented. The male/female couplings presented within the site's imagery are predominantly heteronormative in nature, and further reinforce the long-standing gender binaries of contemporary society.

Further set text help is available for a range of products for all exam boards at www.essentialmediatheory.com

Table 10.1 Speak Judith Butler

Abjection	The process of constructing an object or person as repulsive. Abjection is used, Butler infers, to suggest that non-heteronormative identities are unnatural.
Compulsory heterosexuality	A phrase used by Butler to describe the deeply entrenched social expectation that we assume male/female identities and that we engage in heterosexual relationships.
Gender/sex	Butler differentiates between gender and sex. Gender, she argues, is the socially constructed identity that we assume, while sex refers to the body we are born with.
Gender trouble	A representation or identity that falls outside of heteronormativity. Gender trouble might be inferred through: asexuality, bisexuality, homosexuality, lesbianism, pansexuality, transgenderism or transvestitism. Butler suggests that the performance of gender trouble is a difficult and sometimes painful process.
Gender performance	The repeating of acts or rituals that continuously define our gender. Butler argues that our gender is not innate but constructed through the continuous repetition of micro-rituals.
Gender subversion	A representational process that undermines heteronormativity.
Heteronormativity	The dominance of heterosexuality as a normal or preferred identity – usually accompanied by a view that gender is binary (either male or female).
Parodic representation	An imitative gender representation usually constructed using exaggeration or dissonance. Drag queens are parodic in that they offer us a highly exaggerated version of femininity. Parodic representations can be used to subjugate marginalised identities, but they also simultaneously sketch the performative nature of gender for all of us and are therefore subtly subversive.

Table 10.2 Butler: ten minute revision

Concept 1: *Our gendered identities are not naturally given but constructed through repetition and ritual.*
• Our bodies or sex do not define our gendered identities.
• Genders are not fixed by childhood experiences.
• Gender is constructed through the continuous repetition of micro-rituals.

Concept 2: *Contemporary culture reinforces a traditional gender binary – identities that fall outside of that binary are constructed as subversive.*
• Heteronormativity is entrenched within society.
• Non-heteronormative identities are marginalised or subjugated.
• The media assists in the marginalisation of subversive identities through absent representations, abjection and parody.
• The performance of gender trouble is a difficult, sometimes painful, process given the entrenched nature of heteronormativity.

Two theorists who might challenge Butler's thinking
• **David Gauntlett:** acknowledges much of the work of Butler, but would suggest that contemporary media practices mean that heteronormativity does not completely dominate and that the media allows for diverse or fluid identity construction. He suggests that society has adopted a much more positive view of gender subversion than is presented by Butler.
• **Liesbet van Zoonen:** would agree with Butler's assessment that gender is a social construct but would suggest that the media reinforces male power as a result of women internalising male power and assuming the same passivity that on-screen depictions of femininity construct.

---

11 Media and identity

David Gauntlett

David Gauntlett has been included in the list of prescribed A Level theorists primarily for his work regarding identity theory. Heavily influenced by the thinking of the sociologist Anthony Giddens, Gauntlett constructed a timely critique of mass media consumption models and their effects on audience thinking.

Gauntlett was particularly interested in the impact of the media proliferation boom of the 1980s and 1990s that gave audiences access to more media products and broadcast channels than ever before. The resulting diversity of choice, in Gauntlett's view, fundamentally changed the way that audiences use media products, turning viewers into active rather than passive consumers, and, as a result, giving audiences more control over the way they use the media to craft their identities.

Concept 1: traditional and post-traditional media consumption

Anthony Giddens: traditional and post-traditional culture change

To explain Gauntlett's ideas it is necessary to take a preliminary detour and to explore Anthony Giddens' analysis of the far reaching social changes currently affecting Western societies. We are transitioning, Giddens argues, from a society in which our identities were constructed via rigid traditions to a distinctly different phase that he calls 'late modernity'.

In social structures in which tradition dominates, the notion of who we are is heavily determined by long-standing social forces. The roles that men and women are expected to fulfil, for example, are tightly regulated and heavily moderated by social customs, family expectations and rigid social codes. Thus, cultures based on 'tradition' produce fixed identities that are hard to escape from. Men are expected to assume stereotypically masculine identities, to adopt the role of the primary earner, while women are expected to look after children, to cook for their families and to keep the family home clean. These rigid roles, importantly, are reinforced by the ideological stances taken by wider social institutions such as education, religion and, importantly, the media.

The period that Giddens calls 'late modernity' begins to take shape in the years following the Second World War and is characterised by a relaxation of the rigid social roles expected in a traditionally ordered society. Individuals in 'late modernity' realise, in short, that they can shape their own outlooks and beliefs. This transition is partially enabled, Giddens argues, via the liberating effects of globalisation and by exposing individuals to values and identities that are different to those they experience at the local level.

Globalisation, in brief, allows individuals to transcend the rigid expectations of their immediate communities. By watching, for example, an American soap opera that contains powerful female characters, women in traditionally ordered communities might perceive that an alternative identity exists other than the one that their society has prescribed for them.

Giddens and the reflexive project of the self

As a result, Giddens suggests that individuals who live within 'late modernity' are able to engage in what he calls the 'reflexive project of the self' (Giddens, 1991, 164). The 'self' in 'late modernity' is not fixed, but fluid. In short, we have far more control over who we are in 'late modernity'. We can revise or deconstruct our identities. We can escape the narrow gender or class-based roles prescribed by traditional social structures.

Importantly, David Gauntlett openly acknowledges Giddens' arguments, using them to explore the effects of the contemporary media landscape and arriving at the conclusion that the variety of media products available for us to consume allows us to 'create, maintain and revise a set of biographical narratives – the story of we are, and how we came to be where we are now' (Gauntlett, 2008, 107).

Box 11.1 Discuss it: can you find evidence of social change in your own family?

Giddens suggests that the transition to 'late modernity' accelerated towards the end of the twentieth century. Think about the gender-based roles that your parents and grandparents assume in your own family:

- Who is responsible for cooking, cleaning or childcare in your immediate family? Who goes out to work?
- Do your parents assume traditional or post-traditional gender roles in your immediate family?
- Do your grandparents have a more fixed notion of their gender roles?
- What expectations do you have of yourself and the role you expect to play in your own future family?
- How do your families and your classmates' families compare? Is there evidence to suggest, as Giddens argues, that we are moving from traditionally ordered identities to a less traditional set of expectations?

Concept 2: reflexive identity construction

David Gauntlett: self-help books and consumer led identities

Gauntlett connects Giddens' notion of the 'reflexive project of the self' to the proliferation of media content in the 1980s and 1990s. He argues that the sheer diversity of new products and channels, both niche and mainstream, facilitates the process of identity editing by audiences.

Gauntlett cites the growth of self-help manuals during the 1990s as evidence of our desire to manipulate the way we engage with the world at large. These self-help guides, he tells us, 'describe aspirational but reasonably realistic (as opposed to utopian) models of how we might expect women and men to present themselves in today's society' (Gauntlett, 2008, 233). Self-help books tell us that we do not have to endure the personality flaws that hold us back from the jobs we want or the relationships we desire. A whole new you, whatever that 'you' is, can be realised at the flick of a self-help page found in your local bookshop.

Lifestyle magazines and transformation narratives

Gauntlett suggests that a similar dynamic can be identified in contemporary lifestyle magazines where advice columns and inspiration articles prompt audiences to realise their true callings. The front covers of magazines such as *Vogue* and *Men's Health* are shop windows to a sexier, more successful future-self for their readerships. Inside, lifestyle-oriented contents pages invite their readers to assimilate aspirational ingredients from the diversity of articles and glossy (but not too perfect) imagery that adorns their pages.

Multi-protagonist television and music

In television, too, it could be argued that the arrival of new programme formats in the 1990s facilitated further identity play. Reality television shows of the period drew contestants from a wide social spectrum, asking audiences to reject or embrace candidates based on nothing more than mediated backstories or the narrative journeys those contestants crafted during show transmission. The birth, too, of multi-protagonist TV drama further enhanced the notion that identity was fluid. Where traditional drama formats focused audiences on the identities of a single hero protagonist, multi-protagonist hits such as *Friends* and *Sex and The City* asked audiences to pick their favourite character – to identify with the on-screen presence they felt most akin to. In today's on-demand oriented television landscape, the multi-protagonist drama format rules. From *No Offence* to *The Returned*, most of the television set texts required for exam study contain a rainbow of protagonists that facilitate the same effect.

We might argue that solo music artists have also provided audiences with a set of useful narrative templates as to how identity might be repurposed. Music thrives on identity experimentation, on blurring gender and ethnically-based stereotypes and, in doing so, the music industry has connected impressionable young audiences to a roll call of global stars who have successfully affected identity change. From Michael Jackson's plastic surgery driven resculpting to Beyoncé's regeneration as a radical feminist, the identity U-turns of music artists provide audiences with a streaming narrative of fluidity that they can copy.

Advertising and the alternative you

Likewise, Gauntlett suggests that marketing and advertising agencies construct multiple possibilities of who we might be through product branding, providing us with 30 second glimpses of who we might become – of the ideal versions of ourselves and our loved ones. Of course, we have the power to reject those images, yet, equally, we can also be seduced or inspired by them. These lifestyle narratives, the life-hack impulse of our age, Gauntlett suggests, have gathered further momentum in the digital era – repackaged and repurposed by everyday users in self-penned webzines and DIY YouTube tutorials (Gauntlett, 2008). In the globalised multi-channel media landscape of the late twentieth century, audiences are now in charge of the remote control. Audiences gatekeep the identities they are exposed to and if they do not like what they see they have the power to change channels or, more interestingly, use contemporary digital media platforms to create their own channel.

Box 11.2 Interview with David Gauntlett (January 2019)

MD: Your book Media, Gender and Identity (2002, second edition 2008) was hugely optimistic about the capacity of audiences to use media in shaping their identities. Do you still feel that the contemporary media landscape affords the same opportunities?

DG: Back then, it was still exciting to talk about people using popular culture within the process of constructing their sense of self-identity. But that was people making use of material that was generated by others – a professional elite, essentially.

Nowadays, that sounds awful. The positive thing we have now is the online culture made by everybody, which – while far from perfect – is definitely much richer and more diverse and exciting than what you got from traditional media.

Of course, traditional media still exists and provides us with big, visible slabs of popular culture, which remains a battleground for representations – the questions about who gets represented, and how. But in 2017 I criticised the then new UK A Level syllabus for 'making young people study their grandparents' media preferences', which some teachers seemed to think was harsh, but it's true. The 'mass media' perspective – the shared culture where everyone watches the same stuff – is very twentieth century. It made sense then, but not now. You really want to be talking about the present diverse, digital world.

MD: You are a passionate advocate of digital technologies and their capacity to stimulate a DIY culture. What potential does this culture have to positively transform society?

DG: The basic point I made in *Making is Connecting* (2011, second edition 2018) is that it's always better for people to be making media, and participating in culture, rather than just being a consumer of it. And the arrival of technologies which enable people to do that quite easily, and engage in highly networked conversations around it, makes a fundamental difference to media studies and, more importantly, to our social and cultural life. For too long our cultural conversations were led by the fortunate elite. Now, it's much more open to everyone, which is obviously better. But recently we've seen more of a toxic spiral of social media nastiness – and the mass-surveillance, advertising-driven business model perfected by Facebook – which is awful. We can still get back to a positive, open, DIY culture, I believe, but it'll take a lot of work.

Box 11.3 Apply it: diagnose the ways that set texts encourage identity fluidity

What evidence is in your set texts to reinforce Gauntlett's idea that the media facilitates identity play? Think about the following:

- Do your set texts construct a single ideal identity or do they offer a number of lead characters, presenting the product's audience with a diversity of identities to choose from?
- What versions of gender, ethnicity or class are constructed through the various role models presented in your set texts? Do they reinforce, deconstruct or subvert traditional identities?
- Do your set texts encourage audience identity play? How?

Magazines and online media

- In what ways do the magazines you have studied offer life-changing advice? Which articles promote identity play? What features of readers' lives do the magazines aspire to improve?
- What kinds of aspirational imagery do products present? What effect might ideal imagery have on readers' notions of identity?
- In what ways do the same magazines also construct realism? What is the combined effect of presenting aspiration and realism side-by-side?
- In what ways do the online set texts you have studied offer life advice or deliver role models that their audiences are encouraged to copy?

- How does characterisation, *mise en scène* or language usage reinforce the aspirational nature of the various role models?
- How does the digital presence of contemporary magazines help facilitate identity play? In what ways do magazines encourage audience engagement?
- How does that engagement help audiences to reshape their identity?

Radio

- In what ways do the radio presenters of your radio set texts offer their audiences aspirational role models?
- How does programme content help audiences to reshape or change their real-world lives?

Television and film marketing

- Do set texts offer multiple protagonists? Do these varied protagonists offer a range of identities that audiences can use to inform their own identity construction?
- Do set texts provide aspirational role models?
- Do set texts offer a variety of gender-based representations?
- Do set texts actively deconstruct or question traditional notions of identity?

Gauntlett: the power of media narratives

Gauntlett also draws our attention to the way in which most story structures are concerned with the transformation of a central hero, suggesting that we can 'borrow from these stories when shaping our narratives of the self' (Gauntlett, 2008, 120). In this sense, the characters we watch on television shows or follow in online games offer us examples of how we can transfigure ourselves, of how we can become something better.

Most products provide their fictional leads with character weaknesses or with quests that need to be completed if they are to gain happiness. The journeys those characters take – the challenges they face – might potentially mirror our own weaknesses, or provide us with a template to guide our own goals or desires. At the very least, the transformations offered suggest that our identities are not fixed, but can be altered for the best if we are motivated enough to change who we are.

Box 11.4 Analyse it: identify the impact of narrative transformation in your set texts

Use the following questions to provide three sentence analyses for your set texts to diagnose the effect of character transformation on audience identity:

Fiction-based narratives (TV drama):

- What barriers do central characters face in the wider narratives of the product?
- Do these challenges connect to wider issues of gender, ethnicity, class or ability?
- In what ways does the set text character triumph?
- In what ways do characters transform themselves?
- What are the potential effects of those triumphs on the product's audience?

Non-fiction narratives (magazines, news, radio):

- In what ways do your set texts encourage identity transformation?
- What positive benefits are wrought by transformations?
- What are the potential effects of those narratives on the product's audience?

Use the exemplars below to help structure your responses:

Exemplar 1: *Deutschland 83* (AQA and OCR). Moritz's mission in *Deutschland 83*, to assume the identity of a West German first lieutenant, provides an interesting example of what Gauntlett would call a transformation narrative. Narratives arcs such as these provide audiences with an identity transformation blueprint. The transformation of Moritz in *Deutschland 83*, for instance, is one of liberation, allowing him to transcend the narrow confines of East German society. The text, moreover, reinforces a sense for the audience that their identities are a reflexive project and that they too can revise who they are and escape their own local conditions.

Exemplar 2: *Huck* magazine (Eduqas): Gauntlett suggests that a range of contemporary media products provide readers with transformation blueprints they can use to legitimise identity play. Huck's 'Beyond Binary' feature clearly provides such a template, with Jacob Tobias's self-penned account of his transgender transition offering a clear challenge to fixed notions of traditional gender roles, while also demonstrating the psychological benefits of that transition. Tobias's call to 'work with me' at the end of the article, moreover, is an open invitation to *Huck's* readers to accept gender fluidity as the natural condition of our postmodern age and to similarly affect their own identity-oriented experimentations.

Further set text help is available for a range of products for all exam boards at www.essentialmediatheory.com

Using Gauntlett, van Zoonen and Butler to develop arguments in long format essays

Gauntlett, importantly, is cautious not to overly exaggerate the potential role that the media plays in enabling identity fluidity. He might assert that audiences play an active role in using media to construct non-traditional identities, but he also realises that the weight and scope of traditional representations constructed through media broadcasting do not necessarily enable limitless or very liberated versions of ethnicity or gender.

Gauntlett clearly acknowledges that the media manufactures 'narrow interpretations of certain roles or lifestyles' (Gauntlett, 2008, 113). Yet his conclusions regarding the overriding effect of the contemporary media landscape is a great deal more optimistic than that suggested by van Zoonen or Judith Butler. For Gauntlett, the diversity of representations available to consume via contemporary media contrasts sharply with van Zoonen's assessment that we are controlled by the dominant pull of patriarchy. He also provides a more upbeat assessment than Judith Butler, whose identification of 'gender trouble' as a subversive act conflicts with Gauntlett's optimism. For Gauntlett, 'gender trouble' is not merely a sideshow or a subversive niche. Indeed, contemporary mass media has helped to mainstream non-heteronormativity. (See Table 11.1 for a further comparison of Gauntlett's, van Zoonen's and Butler's representation theories.)

Table 11.1 Quick reference: gender representation theory comparison table

Theorist	Key arguments	Audience effects
van Zoonen	• The media is maintained through patriarchy. • Images of female objectification dominate female representation. • Media makers can challenge dominant representations but those challenges are viewed as subversive. • Calls on media makers to offer subversive representations.	• Audiences are largely passive. • Audiences, both male and female, internalise female objectification. • Audiences reinforce patriarchal ideologies by subconsciously aligning themselves with the values of a male-dominated society.
Judith Butler	• Gender is socially constructed. • Society constructs a binary view of gender (strict roles for males and females). • Society also presents male/female relationships as the norm (heteronormativity). • The media reinforces heteronormativity through heteronormative representations. • Alternatives to the gender binary exist, but are presented as subversive.	• Audiences internalise socially constructed gender norms. • Audiences can seek out representations that offer 'gender trouble'. • Audiences learn how to perform gender via the media. • Audiences can learn alternative models of gender performance – but they are rare and often painfully wrought.
David Gauntlett	• Gender is socially constructed. • We now live in a post-traditional society. • Audiences realise they can change their identities. • The media provides a range of products in which a huge diversity of identities is portrayed. • Alternative lifestyles are becoming mainstream.	• Audiences are active. They control the representations they want to engage with and can actively reject those that do not appeal. • Audiences are free to experiment with a variety of identities. • Audiences use global media to offer alternatives to the identities that society constructs for them.

Table 11.2 Speak David Gauntlett

Active audience engagement	Active audiences are in control of the way they watch or interact with the media. Gauntlett would argue that active audiences use – or make – media products to craft their own identities.
Aspirational narrative	A product that offers a means to self-improvement or offers audiences an ideal lifestyle choice.
Fixed identity	Fixed identities do not give individuals a great deal of choice about who they want to be. Identities might be fixed by religious beliefs, social norms or rigid family roles.
Fluid Identity	Our identities can be described as fluid identities when we realise that they can be changed or that we do not necessarily have to conform to the rigid categories laid down by traditional social structures.
Globalisation	Globalisation, in this chapter, refers to the way that media products began to be produced and shared across the globe as a result of ownership changes in the 1980s. Globalisation brought audiences into contact with a much wider range of identity influences.
Media proliferation	Media proliferation refers to the explosion of media products and channels that started to occur in the early 1980s. Media proliferation meant products were increasingly produced for niche or specialised audiences.
Post-traditional society	A society that does not require individuals to adopt rigid roles or identities.
Reflexive project of the self	A term coined by Anthony Giddens to describe the way that identities are constructed in a post-traditional society. Giddens argues that individuals are able to craft and revise their own identities – that our identities are a constantly evolving and adapting project.
Window to the future self	A product that gives its audience a glimpse into who they could become. Commonly used to describe magazine front covers.

Table 11.3 Gauntlett: ten minute revision

Concept 1: *traditional and post-traditional media consumption*
- Gauntlett's ideas build upon Anthony Giddens' assertion that society has progressed to a stage that Giddens calls 'late modernity'.
- The conditions of late modernity enable audiences to escape the prescriptive identities that are constructed for them through localised social norms and traditional viewpoints.
- Gauntlett argues that contemporary media has brought audiences into contact with a wider range of representations – and, importantly, that audiences can consciously shape their own sense of self.

Concept 2: *reflexive identity construction*
- The media provides a variety of role models and lifestyle templates that audiences use to guide their own outlooks.
- Audiences are engaged in a continuous revision of their identities.
- Media narratives mirror the process of identity transformation.
- Audiences are in control of the media – adapting and assimilating ideas about themselves through the various representations that the media presents.

Three theorists who challenge Gauntlett's thinking
- **Stuart Hall:** would argue that the media landscape is not diverse, but saturated with stereotypical portrayals that reflect wider social inequalities. This leads to a deeply problematic portrayal of minority groups of all persuasions.
- **bell hooks:** hooks would argue that portrayals of black women are largely absent from the media and, when they are present, they are prone to produce overly sexualised portrayals.
- **Paul Gilroy:** would argue that British media narratives do not offer diversity but are stuck within a colonial mindset that positions non-whites as threatening, primitive or uncivilised.

---

12 Ownership effects

James Curran and Jean Seaton

Curran and Seaton's widely read history of the media in the UK, *Power without Responsibility*, is concerned, to a large degree, with narrating the story of how the media landscape has fallen under the control of a handful of global media conglomerates.

Of course, the media landscape has changed considerably since the book's first publication in 1981, and the seventh edition of *Power without Responsibility* (2010) very much reflects contemporary concerns regarding digital media. But at the heart of Curran and Seaton's book remains a core concern – a guiding notion of what the media *ought* to be doing, and it stems, in part, from James Curran's detailed reading of the development of the radical press in the early 1800s.

The numerous radical press pamphlets and small-scale newspapers of the Victorian era, Curran argues, were engines for social and polit ical change. Made by the working class and designed to be read by a working class readership, they highlighted the plight of the poor, and fostered, Curran tells us, 'an alternate value system that symbolically turned the world upside down' (Curran and Seaton, 2010, 15).

The lifespan of this early media form, however, was short lived. A combination of rising production costs and increased competition from high quality, professionally produced titles eventually drove the radical free press out of business. Newspapers of the mid Victorian period, Curran argues, could only be mass produced by those who could afford the extensive start-up costs needed to manufacture products on an industrial scale. Curran, too, points to the corrosive effect of commercial advertising which was sold to offset production costs; the radical press, with its agenda to effect political change, did not partner well with the commercial activities of advertisers who represented the system they wanted to undermine. Without advertising income, the free press could not compete with their commercial rivals, and the process of media concentration – the control of the media by ever larger organisations – began in earnest.

Curran and Seaton suggest that a second and equally turbulent wave of ownership consolidation took place in the latter half of the twentieth century when economic globalisation and the widespread deregulation of the media industry reduced the number of national press titles in the UK to just 11 publications. This lack of diversity, in Curran and Seaton's view, concentrates too much power in the hands of a small number of newspaper proprietors – an entirely different scenario to the news industry's radicalising origins.

Concept 1: media concentration

Creativity versus commerciality

The media industry is driven, Curran and Seaton tell us, by the twin forces of creativity and business. Media creatives – writers, directors, actors and photographers – are tasked to give us exciting, innovative and aesthetically pleasing products, while those we call the media's business managers are responsible for ensuring the profitability and commercial viability of products.

Curran and Seaton suggest that profit-driven motives take precedence over creativity in the world of commercial media – that the agendas of the industry's business managers control creative output. Money wins, while both audience size and audience share determine content. As Jean Seaton explains, 'Commercial broadcasting is based not on the sale of programmes to audiences, but on the sale of audiences to advertisers' (Curran and Seaton, 2010, 90). Because commercial broadcasters need to secure long-term advertising revenue to survive programming, she argues, content is designed to attract economically affluent audiences who are able to buy the products that are promoted during advertising slots.

As a result, peak time television schedules (where commercial space is most sought after and costly) are dominated by lighter entertainment formats, while less popular minority interest products are sidelined to secondary channels or late night slots. Advertising, too, prompts media broadcasters to make content that focuses on capturing an ABC1 demographic – those audiences that can afford to buy the products that advertisers want to sell. 'The reason why,' Curran tells us, 'approximately

Box 12.1 Think about it: the effects of commercial imperatives on set texts

Activity 1: think about advertising effects

Identify which of your set text products are funded through commercial advertising and answer these questions:

- How does advertising affect the content of those products? Are stories sanitised? Are characters stereotyped? Is political content softened?
- In what ways are media products and advertising linked? How does the editorial content in your magazine set texts, for instance, covertly promote the products that are advertised in the magazine?
- Do your commercial set texts serve affluent ABC1 demographics as a result of advertiser needs? In what ways does this need channel content or editorial decisions?

Activity 2: think about audience size effects

- Group your set texts by institution, with commercial products in one group and non-commercial products in another. What do the products in each group have in common? What separates the two groups?
- Are Curran and Seaton right in suggesting that mass audience products tend to be sanitised or lightweight?

Activity 3: think about scheduling

Identify the time of the day that set texts were originally broadcast.

- How do broadcast times affect content?
- What do products broadcast at peak time, 7–10 p.m., have in common?

Activity 4: think about time shifting and on-demand effects

Identify which of your radio/television set texts are distributed as podcasts or through on-demand services.

- What effect does podcasting (time shifting) or on-demand distribution have on the content of set texts? Are products allowed to take more creative risks? Are products more political? More experimental?
- Has on-demand distribution allowed producers to make more niche products?
- What effect does the absence of advertising have on texts produced by Netflix? Do subscription services like these give media creatives more control?

25 per cent of the market sustains half the number of daily [newspaper] titles ... is because this is the most affluent part of the market, and generates a large advertising bounty' (Curran and Seaton, 2010, 90).

Conglomerate advantages

Curran and Seaton also argue that the prohibitive costs and risks associated with the production of media products has resulted in the organisation of media companies into vertically and horizontally aligned conglomerates. Indeed, the success of horizontal and vertical integration means that most commercial print, film and television-based media in America and the UK is now controlled by just six global players: CBS, Comcast, Disney, News Corporation, Time Warner and Viacom.

Horizontal integration

Horizontal integration (HI) occurs when a conglomerate acquires media companies of the same media type. News Corporation is a classic example of a horizontally-aligned organisation in that it owns The *Times*, *The Sunday Times* and *The Sun* news titles in the UK. The benefits of HI can be defined as follows:

- **Production costs can be minimised.** Products can be bought in bulk while production facilities can be brought together to rationalise costs. Owning more than one newspaper title, for example, reduces printing costs through the common ownership of a printing facility or through the bulk buying of paper.
- **Sharing resources.** Horizontally-aligned companies have the power and financial means to develop resources that independent producers are simply unable to develop. The *Times* and *The Sun*, for instance, have developed a social media analysis service called Storyful that investigates and verifies content reported on social media – a resource that helps both titles to detect fake news and to identify trending issues on social media.
- **Controlling the market.** By owning both The *Times* and *The Sun*, News Corporation uses its considerable news gathering resources to control a substantial slice of the broadsheet and tabloid markets in the UK. News Corporation products are also strategically positioned so they do not compete with one other, while

their use of shared resources helps nurture a competitive advantage over rival titles.

Vertical integration

Vertical integration (VI) enables conglomerates to control the production and distribution of media products. Disney is a good example of a vertically integrated company in that it owns subsidiary organisations that fulfil the following aspects of the production process:

- **Production divisions.** Disney owns film production studios (Walt Disney Pictures, Twentieth Century Fox) and television production divisions (Endemol Shine group, ABC).
- **Distribution services.** In owning Sky Plc and Fox Network, Disney are able to globally distribute their filmic and television content without the need to employ external partners. This allows Disney to retain all profits from product distribution and, more importantly, allows full control of where and when content is broadcast.
- **Subsidiary support.** Film and media products need to be financed, promoted and planned – owning specialist support subsidiaries allows Disney to manage projects effectively. For example, Disney uses a variety of specialist subsidiaries including promotional services (Disney Marketing), merchandising (Marvel Toys) and financial/support services (Marvel Film Finance) to help the conglomerate maximise profits.

The advantages of VI include:

- **Capturing upstream and downstream profits.** Producing and distributing products internally creates substantial cost savings. Production subsidiaries do not need to pay distributors to stream their products (thus capturing downstream profits). Likewise, distributor subdivisions do not have to pay external providers for media content (thus capturing upstream profits).
- **Control over all aspects of the production chain.** Owning a satellite network means Disney can release products in ways that maximise profits. Sky subscribers, for instance, are given access to premium movie content during the lucrative Christmas holiday

period. VI also allows companies to release or schedule products so that they do not compete with one another.

• **Restricting access to competitors.** By controlling key distribution outlets, Disney can prevent rivals from dominating broadcast schedules and can even charge rivals who wish to distribute their products through Disney owned networks.

• **Cross-media ownership synergies.** Owning a variety of media company types enables the conglomerate to distribute product benefits across a range of media forms. For instance, Marvel Television uses the advanced production processes developed for Marvel Films. Characters and storylines developed for the *Star Wars* film franchise can also be recycled into gaming products.

Box 12.2 Think about it: the effect of horizontal and vertical integration on set texts

Use the following questions to identify the effects of horizontal and vertical integration on set texts:

Activity 1: diagnosing vertical integration effects

• How do ownership patterns help in terms of product distribution? What distribution services does the conglomerate own? How do these distribution channels give the product access to mass audiences?

• How do distribution subsidiaries help the set text reach a global audience? How does this increase the profitability of the product?

• What effect does the set text's distribution have on budget constraints? Because the set text is distributed to a mass audience does it have a bigger budget than it would if made by an independent?

• Do cross-media ownership patterns give the set text an opportunity to be translated into other media formats?

Activity 2: diagnosing horizontal integration effects

• Does the product serve a clearly defined target audience as a result of HI ownership patterns? What audiences do sister companies target? Are audiences differentiated to maximise profits?

• How does the set text use the shared expertise/joint resources of a sister company to make or distribute the product?

Concept 2: effects of concentration on media content

Proprietor control of print news

Media concentration has resulted in the elevation of proprietor power. Media owners, Curran argues, control the content and flow of news either directly or indirectly:

- **Direct control.** Proprietor owners, Curran suggests, censor news content that conflicts with their political views and wider business interests. Generally speaking, large-scale conglomerates that own news titles also have vested interests in a range of other business activities all over the globe – banking, engineering, oil and transport – that their media divisions are directed to ignore if conflicts of interest arise.

- **Indirect control** of news content might also be affected through the hiring and firing process, through the installation of editors who are sympathetic to a specific worldview that a proprietor wants to broadcast.

Elitist media/political relationships

Curran also draws our attention to the relationships that have developed between news groups, big business and government, suggesting that the power of concentrated media ownership has forced political parties to form cosy relationships with media moguls in order to get favourable press coverage.

The former Labour Prime Minister, Tony Blair, for example, was famously invited to address News Corporation executives in 1995 before he was elected, while Murdoch's relationship with Margaret Thatcher during the 1980s was close enough, reportedly, that he could affect some influence over crucial policy decisions regarding media regulation. Curran suggests, rather powerfully, that these cosy relationships result in the formation of a news landscape that lacks the critical bite of a fully functioning press establishment.

Mass market news, news depoliticisation and hysterical news values

Media concentration has significantly reduced the diversity of available news titles, while at the same increasing the readerships of those titles that remain. Catering for the needs of those huge readerships, Curran argues, has resulted in a watering down of news content. Mass readership newspapers are depoliticised as a result – often replacing hard news with entertainment-driven content, while the quality and tone of news coverage is sensationalised in a bid to retain audience share.

Curran and Seaton: a Neo-Marxian approach?

Curran and Seaton suggest that contemporary media ownership places the media in the hands of the few and not the many. In this sense, they take an approach that follows in the footsteps of the Victorian economist and philosopher Karl Marx. Marx argued that culture – the arts and so forth – is deployed to make the working poor believe that there is not really much alternative to the drudgery of their appalling working conditions. Marx argued that:

- **Culture is controlled by social elites.** Curran and Seaton likewise suggest the media is controlled by a minority of wealthy institutions and that those institutions often work for the benefit of themselves.
- **Culture acts as a distraction.** Culture, according to Marx, provides a temporary escape from the drudgery of our working lives and, in doing so, it distracts us from true nature of our exploitation. Curran and Seaton would similarly argue that the media offers us depoliticised narratives through entertainment-oriented media that is highly formulaic.

Regulated media pluralism

Yet, to label Curran and Seaton as nothing more than neo-Marxists would miss much of the thrust of their work. They might call out press proprietor abuses, but they also present a strong case for what might loosely be termed 'media pluralism', arguing that the media landscape ought to be populated by a range of company types, both commercial and public service oriented.

Box 12.3 Apply it: media concentration and news-based set texts

This activity is particularly useful for exam-based questions that ask you identify the effects of ownership on set text news products. Analyse relevant set texts using the following prompts:

- Curran suggests that contemporary newspapers have to compete for readers' interests, often using hysterical news values – making them angry or frightened – to attract and sustain mass readerships. In what ways do your news set texts support this argument?
- Is political coverage minimised or sensationalised in contemporary news?
- Does the editorial mix of contemporary print news feature an unusually large element of softer news features, sports coverage or entertainment-based coverage?
- Do the editorial biases of your set text newspapers reflect the political views of their proprietors?
- In what ways do set text newspapers rely on official sources for stories? Do they readily challenge those sources or accept them as accurate?
- Are journalists and columnists given the freedom to express ideas that conflict with proprietor views?
- Do newspapers incorporate reader commentary and opinion to broaden the perspectives offered?

Exemplar: *The Daily Mail* (OCR). *The Daily Mail* exemplifies much of the thrust of Curran and Seaton's arguments regarding the effect of media concentration on news reportage. Media globalisation, they argue, has resulted in the domination of the industry by a handful of politically motivated proprietor owned titles that are dependent on advertising and mass audience readership to remain commercially viable. A mass marketisation of news has resulted, Curran tells us, using hysterical news values and softer news content to maintain mass appeal in the face of cut-throat competition. *The Daily Mail* front cover of 17 February 2018 provides ample evidence of both trends. The now discredited and sensationalist headline 'Corbyn the Collaborator' invokes hysteria and fear, and, in so doing, sacrifices objective journalism in favour of the overt political bias of the newspaper's proprietor. Moreover, the competition strapline positioned above the leader exchanges prime front page space for advertising as a result of *The Daily Mail's* need to target a commercially lucrative ABC1 demographic. The lifestyle-oriented advertorial also evidences the paper's softer editorial mix – a clear effect of the need to provide content that has mass-market appeal.

Further exemplars for set texts from all exam boards are available online at: www.essentialmediatheory.com

Certainly, Curran and Seaton highlight the need to protect UK public service broadcasting to counterbalance the forces of the free market. In this sense, they are media pluralists, suggesting that media audiences are served best when a range of different institutions contribute to the media landscape.

The internet and ownership concentration

Certainly, there was much to celebrate at the outset of the internet's invention in terms of its potential to challenge the top-down nature of traditional media. Yet, Curran and Seaton suggest, the web landscape of today is increasingly commercialised, with large-scale traditional media companies having invested huge amounts of time and money to develop equally huge web presences. These companies, Curran tells us, 'had enormous assets: back catalogues of content, large reserves of cash

---

Box 12.4 Think about it: the creeping commercialisation of the web

Do your online set texts provide evidence that the radical potential of the internet has been curtailed by commercial pressures?

Questions to test the level of commercialisation of online set texts

- Which parent companies make your online set texts – are they part of an established media conglomerate? Have producers partnered up with commercial organisations to make their product?
- Is the online set text financed, either wholly or in part, by commercial advertising? What is the potential effect of advertising on the content of the product?
- Does the set text openly, or even covertly, market products to its audience?

Questions to diagnose public service benefits of online set texts

- Do your online set texts invite commentary from its users? Is commentary designed to prompt debate?
- Do set texts give marginalised groups a voice?
- Do products foreground information over product sales?
- Are products designed to nurture an online community?

and expertise, close links with the advertising industry, brand visibility and cross promotional resources' (Curran and Seaton, 2010, 265). As a result, the natural advantages of media conglomerates meant that they were able to affect a sizeable web presence very quickly. In 1996, the internet was a relatively advert free interface; fast forward 20 years and we barely register the presence of all those web cookies logging our browsing activity. Facebook mines our personal data so that we might be sold to advertisers. YouTube monetises user uploads, turning cat videos and vlogs into spaces that can be prefaced by adverts for soft drinks, cars and hair products. The web has become a place of commerce rather than a space to share and discuss. But, Curran argues, the web is still a contested space. Enough cyber mavericks exist, he suggests, to ensure that the world's digital networks have not been completely overtaken by major corporations just yet.

Concept 3: diverse ownership creates diverse products

The free market effect

UK government policy, Seaton and Curran argue, is responsible, in part, for the widespread domination of the media landscape by huge conglomerates. Jean Seaton points to the prevailing neo-liberal viewpoint of politicians who were in charge of media policy from the 1980s onwards, with both Labour and Conservative ministers championing a 'free market' media landscape. Free market neo-liberalism is intended to produce, in Jean Seaton's words, 'conditions of the greatest possible competition' (Curran and Seaton, 2010, 371), in which media audiences determine content, not politicians, and where companies that provide the most popular content are allowed to flourish without government sponsored restrictions.

Commercial media provision has exploded as a result of neo-liberal policy making. In 1980, just 300 weekly hours of television programming were broadcast, yet, by the year 2000, that number had grown to over 40,000 hours (Curran and Seaton, 2010, 246). The problem, Curran and Seaton highlight, is that without suitable controls, commercial media companies readily abandon commitments to public service broadcasting and content diversity. We might have more television content, they argue, but the pursuit of mass audience appeal has produced a landscape that is dominated by format-driven products.

Media formats that are successful are replicated to deliver mass audiences. *The Great British Bake Off*, for instance, morphed into *The Great British Sewing Bee*, while the dominance of prime time talent shows such as *The Voice* and *Britain's Got Talent* have spawned a stream of shows that share remarkably similar formats. Channel 4, too, mines formats relentlessly – *24 Hours in Police Custody*, *24 Hours in A&E*, *Countdown*, *8 out 10 Cats Does Countdown*, etc. The need to produce mass audiences means that the television industry replicates rather than originates.

One might argue that the explosion of streaming giants such as Netflix has helped break the formulaic approach taken by terrestrial television broadcasters; yet, even here, the use of audience data drives Netflix commissioning processes. New content is routinely devised on the basis that storylines replicate the popularity of pre-existing narratives. Far from increasing consumer choice, media proliferation, in this sense, has given us products that lack invention.

Public service broadcasting as a counter influence to commercial media

Commercial media has not been allowed to dominate UK television and radio markets completely. The BBC, as a public service broadcaster funded through the television licence fee, operates without the

---

Box 12.5 Think about it: is the media dominated by format-driven products?

Curran and Seaton suggest that commercial media broadcasters copy rival products that are successful or rely on trusted television formats to deliver safe programming. Think about the following questions to test the truth of Curran and Seaton's arguments today:

- In what ways do the schedules of major broadcasters offer similar products during peak viewing slots?
- Can you think of some examples of television programmes/formats that have been successful and have produced copycat products as a result of that success?
- How far do you agree with the argument that streaming services like Netflix rely on a formulaic approach?

need to attract advertising revenue to fund programming. This guaranteed funding structure has garnered the criticism of many free market advocates, some of whom have championed a root and branch scaling back of the BBC to stimulate further commercial media expansion. Yet, the BBC remains ever popular – its reach and diversity securing enough public support to ward off any far-reaching or life-threatening reforms.

Curran and Seaton (2010) put forward the following four benefits that derive from the BBC's unique funding status:

- **Programming standards are raised.** Because the BBC is not part of a larger cross-industry conglomerate it approaches news with impartiality. The BBC's impartial approach also sets high standards that other broadcasters emulate.
- **High-quality minority interest programming is provided.** Without the need to make a profit, the BBC can serve minority audience interests through programming and scheduling. The BBC's commitment to the arts, for instance, is evidenced via BBC 4, while minority ethnic and regional audiences are engaged through the BBC Asian Network as well as BBC Wales with its heavy commitment to regional news and radio. (See Box 12.6 for more discussion on how BBC Radio creates appeal for niche audiences.)
- **It is a unifying organisation.** The BBC's focus is not trained on the advertising bonanzas achieved by targeting an ABC1 demographic. The BBC, as a public service broadcaster, is inclusive rather than exclusive.

Box 12.6 Revise it: BBC Radio and public service broadcasting

BBC Radio output provides an excellent illustration of the organisation's non-commercial remit to inform, educate and entertain. With 10 national radio stations and over 40 local stations, the BBC provides a range of niche and majority interest radio programming. Freed from profit-driven motives, the BBC can also deliver a diversity of content that would not ordinarily survive if it were funded through advertising.

Exemplar: Radio 4 and *Late Night Woman's Hour* (Eduqas). Radio 4 is one of only a few UK-based radio stations that are dominated by spoken word broadcasting. *Woman's Hour* is dedicated to a female listenership, while the show's evening spin-off, *Late Night Woman's Hour* (LNWH), targets a tighter third wave feminist niche audience with its politically charged debate format.

Issues that you could relate to Curran and Seaton in an exam might include:

- **The programme's format:** listeners are offered a broadcast that focuses on a single topic, facilitating detailed and informative discussion.

- **Guest diversity:** Panellists are invited from a range of cultural, professional and academic backgrounds to promote a detailed consideration of a wide range of third wave feminist viewpoints.

- **Minority issue debate:** The show focuses on minority issues not normally covered in commercial media.

- **Choice of presenter:** Lauren Laverne reflects the educated, career-oriented thirtysomething niche audience of LNWH. This niche audience, importantly, could not be served by a mainstream media organisation reliant on advertising.

Further set text help is available for a range of products for all exam boards at www.essentialmediatheory.com

Table 12.1 Speak Curran and Seaton

Commercial media	An organisation that makes or distributes products for economic gain. Commercial media usually make products for entertainment purposes.
Horizontal integration	Ownership of subsidiaries that produce similar types of products.
Hysterical news values	Sensationalist news content used to drive mass market sales.
Mass market news	News designed to appeal to huge readerships, often critiqued for its lack of analysis or entertainment-driven values. Also known as news depoliticisation.
Media concentration/ media convergence	A term used to describe the reduction in the number of media organisations that produce products.
Media pluralism	A media landscape with a healthy balance of products made by different media company types. Typically these company types include public service broadcasters, commercial media and citizen-generated media.
Public service broadcasting	A media producer who is not reliant on advertising to fund production or does not make products for commercial gain. Public service broadcasting products usually seek to inform and educate their audiences as well entertain.
Vertical integration	Ownership of subsidiaries that enable a media producer to produce, promote and distribute products.

Table 12.2 Curran and Seaton: ten minute revision

Concept 1: *the media is controlled by a small number of companies that make products to create profit*
- Globalisation has concentrated media ownership into the hands of a few companies.
- Media conglomerates are horizontally and vertically integrated to maximise profit.
- Large-scale media producers rely on advertising to generate income.
- Advertising drives media companies to produce products that have mass audience appeal.

Concept 2: *media concentration adversely affects media content*
- The business function of the media industry takes precedence over its creative/public service capacities.
- Profit-driven media is softened to create mass audience appeal.
- Minority interest content is pushed to the margins of broadcast schedules.
- Free market competition produces format-driven products.

Concept 3: *diverse ownership creates diverse products*
- Curran and Seaton highlight the damage that free market ideologies have had on the media landscape.
- Public service broadcasting provides impartial news, serves minority audiences and champions national unity by offering inclusive rather than exclusive content.

Three theorists who might challenge Curran and Seaton's thinking
- **Clay Shirky:** argues that the media industry is increasingly driven by audience feedback systems rather than the top-down control of proprietors.
- **Henry Jenkins:** would acknowledge that Web 2.0 enables big business to exploit the web for commercial reasons, but would also argue that the internet retains the capacity to work as a social good and that online communities created via 'participatory culture' have the power to change the world for the better.
- **Steve Neale:** would critique the idea that media proliferation has resulted in a narrowing of product type or the dominance of formula-driven media. He would argue that audiences prompt producers to continuously adapt and finesse genre-driven material.

---

13 Regulation

Sonia Livingstone and Peter Lunt

Sonia Livingstone and Peter Lunt's academic work constructs a critical analysis of the changing regulatory landscape in the UK over the last 30 years. Central to that analysis is an exploration of how the UK's approach to media governance has served the needs of audiences as both consumers and citizens.

Consumer-based regulation, Livingstone and Lunt tell us, is realised, first, through the creation of a media landscape in which audiences can choose the sorts of media content they can or want to watch and, second, by giving media producers the freedom to create products that those audiences choose to consume. A consumer-based regulatory framework, in short, seeks to guarantee audience choice and promote product diversity.

Conversely, a citizen-based view argues that the media ought to play a significant role in shaping society and its citizens – that television, newspapers, radio, etc. ought to educate and inform their audiences, while also performing a pivotal function in maintaining the democratic health of the nation that producers operate within. Governments and government policy, importantly, play a critical role in defining the kinds of content that the media ought to broadcast or publish in a citizen-oriented regulatory framework.

Crucially, in Livingstone and Lunt's view the media policies affected by successive governments over the last 20 years have worked in ways that have protected, by and large, the commercial interests of media producers.

Concept 1: citizen and consumer models of media regulation

The consumer-oriented approach

A consumer-based regulatory approach offers the following advantages and features:

- **Regulation champions consumer choice.** Consumer-orientated regulation is designed, principally, to encourage media plurality and to ensure that a diversity of broadcasters operate within the media landscape. A consumer-led market allows audiences to be able to access a broad range of content, opinions and ideas.
- **Relies on consumer-led policing of programme content.** Content monitoring, Livingstone and Lunt argue, plays a secondary role within a consumer-based regulatory model, with audiences having to 'rely much more on their own judgements of quality, truthfulness and enjoyment' (Livingstone and Lunt, 2012, 16).
- **The state plays a minor role in determining media regulation.** A consumer-based regulatory model minimises the role that government plays in pushing media providers to make content that has specific benefits – news, factual programming, educational content for children, etc. The media's central role is to make content that is consumer led and not determined by government-led quotas or overbearing content codes.

The citizen-based approach

In contrast, the citizen-oriented approach provides the following features and advantages:

- **Constructs a media model based on civic republicanism.** Livingstone and Lunt argue that citizen-based regulation provides a content focused framework that directs media makers to 'contribute to the enrichment of cultural and social life and the potential for self-development of individuals, groups and communities' (Livingstone and Lunt, 2012, 39). Civic-minded media providers serve audiences not just with entertainment-based content, but also with education and information. Moreover, the civic republicanism model directs media producers to serve a diversity of audience types, both mainstream and minority, niche and broad.

Box 13.1 Discuss it: do you favour a consumer-based or citizen-based approach?

- Should media producers be compelled to provide educational content?
- Should we censor media content so that audiences are protected from seeing material that is offensive? To what degree should the government play a role in deciding what we should or should not watch?
- Should the media play a significant role in reinforcing democracy? What might happen if the media did not inform us through political coverage?

- **Citizen-based regulation foregrounds content issues.** Maintaining acceptable standards of content is a primary focus for citizen-based regulation. Content makers are tasked to ensure that accuracy is maintained and that programmes deal with issues in a fair and objective manner.
- **Encourages a media landscape that can critique governmental power.** Livingstone and Lunt argue that a central function of the media sector, if it is working properly, lies in its ability to hold the government and other sources of authority to account.

Communications Act 2003

The Communications Act 2003 was designed by the then Labour government to modernise the UK's regulatory systems and help the UK television industry become competitive in the globalised media landscape of the late twentieth century. The 2003 Act, among other things, promoted independent television production by requiring the BBC and Channel 4 to commission more content from smaller production companies.

Crucially, for Livingstone and Lunt, the replacement of the Broadcast Standards Commission (BSC) and the Independent Television Commission (ITC) with the new super regulator Ofcom through the Communications Act 2003 significantly diluted the public service requirements of television broadcasting. As a result, independent television production companies were freed up to produce content that was more commercially viable, but this also resulted, some critics suggest, in the production of programming that lacks the civic-minded republicanism that had been fostered within previous regulatory frameworks. Livingstone and Lunt argue that Ofcom 'established institutional structures and roles relating to consumer policy ... Strikingly, little equivalent activity or accountability was forthcoming regarding actions to further citizen interests' (Livingstone and Lunt, 2012, 50).

More general criticism is levelled at the UK's current regulatory infrastructure regarding the way that the various bodies that are responsible for media oversight are managed. The organisations tasked to regulate the media are overseen, by and large, by staff who are drawn from the very industries they seek to police, prompting accusations of industry bias, while the codes of practice enforced are further criticised as light touch – existing, to a large extent, to protect the interests of vulnerable audiences and children.

Self-regulation

In the absence of state guidance, media producers are left, to a large degree, to independently decide upon their own moral or ethical codes of production. As a result, most media organisations construct their own editorial codes to guide the creative personnel working under their remit. Of course, these editorial codes vary enormously from one institution to the next. *The Daily Star*, for instance, adopts a much looser approach to sexually explicit content than *The Guardian*, while the BBC's commitment to producing citizen-oriented content is far more extensive than its commercial rivals. Broadcasters and publishers will invariably use the following factors to help them define the editorial standards that their output should maintain:

- **Independent regulator codes of conduct:** most producers will apply the editorial codes of their sector-based regulator (see Table 13.1).
- **Audience-based factors:** producers and editors are sensitive to the needs and tastes of their target audiences.
- **Advertiser needs:** commercial producers are also mindful of the impact that editorial content will have on advertising revenues. Advertisers invariably place adverts in products that match their own brand values and will readily pull advertising if content does not match their own ethical steer.
- **Institution-oriented factors:** some organisations – the BBC and Channel 4 in particular – are obliged to provide citizen-oriented content as a result of their broadcasting licence agreements.

Table 13.1 Quick reference: key regulators operating in the UK

Regulator	Responsible for	Primary responsibilities
Ofcom	• Commercial radio and television. • Video on demand (NOW TV, Amazon Prime but not Netflix or YouTube). • Jointly responsible for regulating the BBC alongside the BBC's board of governors.	• Tries to ensure that the media landscape is not dominated by a single organisation. • Oversees complaints from members of the public. • Protect those under 18 years old from exposure to harmful content.
Advertising Standards Authority (ASA)	• Print advertising (newspapers, magazines). • Ambient advertising (billboards, bus hoardings). • Radio advertising. • Television advertising. • Internet advertising (including YouTube). • Social media content in which online advertisers promote products.	• Oversees complaints made by members of the public regarding adverts. • Applies a standards code – mostly concerned with protecting vulnerable groups and to ensure accuracy in advert claims. • Pre-clears screen-based advertising. • Encourages self-regulation.
Independent Press Standards Organisation (IPSO)	• Regulates a voluntary membership of over 1,500 print (newspaper and magazines) and 1,000 online news titles. • Some newspapers have refused to sign up to the voluntary code, including *The Guardian*, *The Observer* and *The Financial Times*.	• The semi-official press regulator for the UK – oversees reader complaints that infringe its editorial code of conduct. • Has the power to levy fines of up to £1 million, but, in practice, has never issued any financial penalties. • Complaints are overseen by an adjudicating panel made up of industry based experts.

continued

Table 13.1 Continued

Regulator	Responsible for	Primary responsibilities
British Board of Film Classification (BBFC)	• UK film and video distribution. • Adult internet content.	• Operates a co-regulatory code that classifies films according to age appropriate criteria. • The key focus of the BBFC is to protect children from harmful content and to help parents make informed viewing choices for their children.
Pan European Game Information (PEGI)	• Console and PC games including console-related online gaming content. • Games developers self-certify their own content using the PEGI classification system.	• Operates a content code that enables age related classification of games. • Like the BBFC, PEGI's primary aim is to provide reliable information to guide parents when purchasing console games.

Box 13.2 Apply it: using Livingstone and Lunt to answer regulation-oriented questions

Livingstone and Lunt suggest that the UK is dominated by a consumer-based approach to regulation. Regulation impacts on products in the following ways:

1   A consumer-oriented regulatory approach has created product diversity in which audiences play a vital role in regulating their own media consumption.

2   Media producers are trusted to police their own content (guided by the 'light-touch' editorial codes of independent regulators).

3   Some media producers choose to include citizen-oriented content – social diversity, educational elements, etc. – as a result of following a public service broadcasting ethos.

4   Consumer-oriented regulatory codes exist, primarily, to protect vulnerable audiences.

5   Media producers face light-touch sanctions when editorial codes are infringed.

Use the following questions to help guide your analysis of the consumer impact:

Consumer choice

- Does the product contain material that is controversial?
- In what ways does set text content meet the demands of the target audience?

Self-regulatory effects and citizen-oriented content

- In what ways does the set text police its own content? What prompts this self-policing?
- How do target audience/advertiser needs affect self-regulatory decisions?
- Does the product deliberately contain material that exemplifies a civic-minded approach? Why?

Protection of vulnerable audiences

- How do the set texts protect vulnerable users from content?
- Does the set text broadcast content that contains material that is problematic for vulnerable users? How?
- In what ways does the set text comply with regulatory codes to protect vulnerable audiences?

Infringement issues

- Has the set text ever infringed regulatory guidelines? What were the repercussions of those infringements?

Exemplar: Broadsheet news titles (all exam boards). Livingstone and Lunt's argument that the media landscape is dominated by a consumer-based regulatory system can certainly be applied to the newspaper sector. The Independent Press Standards Organisation (IPSO) oversees news and magazine standards in the UK but, many would argue, exercises a light-touch regime that is weighted in favour of producers (rather than their audiences) as a result of press domination of IPSO's governing body – with members often drawn from the newspaper industry rather than the wider public. IPSO's editorial code, however, does outline clear standards for the press – these are mostly concerned with editorial accuracy and the need to protect vulnerable members of the public, while infringements of the code can incur a £1 million fine. IPSO, however, has never levied any financial penalty, while a number of newspapers have refused to sign up to IPSO's editorial code (including *The Guardian*).

In the absence of an effective citizen-based regulatory framework, *The Guardian*, *The Telegraph* and *The Independent* have all individually developed their own exacting codes of conduct. These codes, of course, reinforce brand integrity, reassuring consumers and advertisers that they can maintain trust in the news gathering activities of broadsheets. But they also outline, in Livingstone and Lunt's words, an ethical commitment to 'civic republicanism' and to use their products in ways that seek to enrich our lives. We might have a light-touch regulatory system, but the institutional perspectives of the broadsheet sector have enabled news gathering in the UK to maintain a citizen-oriented bias.

Further set text help is available for a range of products for all exam boards at www.essentialmediatheory.com

Concept 2: regulation in the globalised media age

Livingstone and Lunt tell us that the global nature of contemporary media production and distribution has weakened the UK's ability to effect meaningful control of media content. Indeed, producers that broadcast their products from outside of UK are largely exempt from the reach of domestic regulatory bodies that oversee content standards. Netflix stands as a useful exemplar here in that its America-based distribution system means that it is exempt from Ofcom control.

A similar regulatory challenge is produced by online media content. The failure of the Communications Act 2003 to address online material and the reluctance of UK governments to tackle the issue since then has prompted widespread dissatisfaction. The difficulties of internet regulation stem from the following:

- **The relatively recent expansion of online services.** Today's tech giants have expanded their reach at an extraordinary rate. Anticipating and reacting to the regulatory issues thrown up by that expansion has been hugely difficult.
- **Tech giants do not author their own content.** Because Facebook, YouTube and Twitter publish user generated content it makes it almost impossible for them to pre-vet problematic material. YouTube, for instance, claims to have over one billion users with some estimates suggesting that over 300 hours of footage are uploaded every minute. Companies have had some

---

Box 13.3 Discuss it: should the internet be regulated?

- What evidence can you present to support the argument that the internet should be regulated?
- Have you ever seen any problematic online content?
- Does the internet pose a particular problem for vulnerable users? In what ways?

---

success in deploying content-vetting algorithms to automate their gatekeeping processes, but they currently lack the sophistication to solve meaningful regulatory issues in a satisfactory way.

- **Online media providers lie beyond the reach of UK regulation.** Much like Netflix, regulation of the internet's major content producers is made more difficult because their operations are based outside of UK.
- **The internet is decentralised.** Attempts to regulate social media giants may succeed, but regulation of the wider content of the net is a hugely difficult task given the extent of material available and the number of authors manufacturing content.
- **Online anonymity.** The anonymous authoring of content also makes it hard to identify individuals and to take meaningful action if content contravenes expectations.

Table 13.2 Apply it: diagnosing the impact of institutional context on regulation

Medium	Key themes
Television and radio	• **Self-regulation and the BBC.** BBC products exemplify a civic-minded approach to production, readily applying a citizen-based ethos to their products. • **Self-regulation and Channel 4.** Channel 4 was initially constructed as a public service broadcaster, and still retains much of that civic-minded ethos, yet a combination of budgetary constraints and a reliance on advertising has pushed the broadcaster towards what many would regard as a consumer-based production agenda, As a result, Channel 4 increasingly commissions content that promotes entertainment values over public service.

continued

Table 13.2 Continued

Medium	Key themes
	• **Increased competition for terrestrial broadcasters from global media.** Some would argue that the relatively weak regulatory approach by the UK government in terms of protecting UK content has allowed global media producers to dominate UK television viewing. The European Union, in contrast, is setting a 30 per cent quota to ensure that streaming providers make European content. • **Netflix.** Netflix is exempt from UK regulatory control. Netflix productions, moreover, is driven by audience data, with successful programmes and genres providing the creative steer for new shows. In this sense, Netflix operates a model of content production that is consumer driven. Netflix, too, has been criticised for its loose editorial approach, with shows like *13 Reasons Why* attracting considerable censure for its on-screen treatment of teenage suicide.
Newspapers and magazines	• **Weak press regulation.** The failure of the Communications Act 2003 to include the print news sector within the remit of Ofcom is seen to be particularly problematic. The creation of IPSO in the wake of the Leveson Inquiry, moreover, has prompted a great deal of criticism regarding the new regulator's failure to encourage citizen-based news values across the print sector. • **Broadsheet self-regulation.** Broadsheet newspapers, however, have tried to maintain their reputations by constructing their own citizen-oriented editorial codes.
Online	• **Limited regulation of online content.** The failure of the Communications Act 2003 to address internet-based content has resulted in a regulatory approach to online media that is relatively weak. Social media, in particular, lacks effective regulation. • **Online extremism.** The failure of social media to control fake news and extremist content is the result of a regulatory model that does not adequately take account of audiences as citizens.

Medium	Key themes
	• **Protecting vulnerable users.** The capacity for social media to influence youth audiences is particularly concerning. Instagram's inability, in 2018, to remove content that encouraged teenage suicides prompted significant censure. • **Regulating online influencers.** The ASA, however, does regulate online advertising and has taken action to make sure that online influencers who endorse products through YouTube, Snapchat and Twitter declare any payments received to their followers. • **The difficulties of policing global online media.** Online media provides a further difficulty in that most content is delivered by tech giants who fall beyond the reach of the UK's regulatory system. The power and size of online media giants makes it incredibly difficult for the UK government to create applicable legislation.
Film and gaming	• **The creation of advisory bodies designed to protect vulnerable audiences.** Both the BBFC and PEGI play an advisory role in terms of informing parents about the content of products. In the case of gaming, the application of PEGI codes has had a limited effect on controlling the sale of problematic content to children.

Table 13.3 Speak Livingstone and Lunt

Citizen-based regulation	Citizen-based regulatory systems outline a civic role for the media and encourage media makers to produce content that contributes to the social and cultural health of the societies in which they operate.
Consumer-based regulation	A regulatory system in which choices regarding content are largely devolved to audiences and where media makers are given as much freedom as possible to make the media that audiences want to consume.
Digital literacy	Sonia Livingstone advocates that audiences should be adequately informed about online content in a way that allows them to effectively evaluate the material they are presented with online.
Self-regulation	Self-regulation devolves regulatory decisions to industry practitioners.

Table 13.4 Livingstone and Lunt: ten minute revision

Concept 1: *citizen and consumer based models of media regulation*
• Citizen-oriented regulation is concerned with content-based issues.
• Citizen-based regulation is a positive form of regulation that directs media content so that it can improve the lives of citizens and contribute to the well-being of wider society.
• Citizen-based regulation promotes forms of media that are able to hold powerful groups to account.
• Consumer-based regulation seeks to ensure that the media landscape contains a variety of different producers so that audiences have choice.
• Consumer-based regulation seeks to ensure that the technological infrastructure that provides media to the public is fit for purpose.
• Consumer-based regulation creates an environment in which audiences themselves make judgements about the kinds of media that are appropriate for their consumption.
• A consumer-oriented approach has dominated the media landscape as a result of the Communications Act 2003 and the creation of Ofcom.

Concept 2: *the challenge of regulation in the age of globalised media*
• Globalisation has reduced the power of national governments to control the media – global companies operate beyond the scope and boundaries of any one country.

Two theorists who might challenge Livingstone and Lunt
• **Henry Jenkins:** would emphasise the benefits that the global digital media landscape offers. He would argue that digital media allows audiences to freely construct their own products and to make connections with like-minded individuals across the world. This process has also enabled some groups to affect deep-seated social change.
• **David Gauntlett:** again, would emphasise the benefits of globalisation. Globalisation, he might argue, has brought audiences into contact with a wide range of identities that they did not previously have access to. This has helped audiences to perceive their identities as fluid and not fixed.

---

14 The culture industry

David Hesmondhalgh

Hesmondhalgh's 'cultural industries' approach explores the media from the perspective of commercial production practices and makes two enormously important observations regarding the necessities of product development:

1. **Products exist as a result of their economic context.** Hesmondhalgh, first and foremost, tells us that media products are made within a commercial context. Much like any other business product, media content is manufactured to create profit, or, in the case of public service broadcasting, to maintain audience engagement. To gain a full understanding of the media industry and its impacts, Hesmondhalgh argues, we must appreciate the extent to which media-making decisions are guided by the needs of commerce as opposed to creativity.

2. **The media industry is a high risk business.** 'All business is risky,' Hesmondhalgh writes, 'but the cultural industries constitute a particularly risky business' (Hesmondhalgh, 2015, 27). The impossibility of predicting audience tastes coupled with the high costs of production and the effects of mass competition mean that the business of making commercially successful media is very difficult. The reduction of those risks, Hesmondhalgh argues, has compelled the media industry to be structured in highly specific ways with risk minimisation, moreover, playing a crucial role in directing the design and marketing of media content.

Concept 1: maximising profits and minimising risks

The high stakes nature of the media industry is exemplified, perhaps, by the enormous problems that film production companies face when trying to distribute a new release. *Forbes* magazine estimates that of the 700 plus films released in cinemas during 2018, over 80 per cent lost money. Similarly, the British Film Institute's analysis of the 760 films released in the UK in 2017 identifies that the top 50 grossing releases took 81 per cent of box office takings, while the bottom 660 films shared just 7 per cent of audience receipts (BFI, 2018).

Such figures underline the 'winner takes all' nature of commercial media, in which a relatively small number of big hits capture a disproportionate share of the available profits. Predicting the success of those big hits, Hesmondhalgh tells us, is hugely difficult if not impossible. Hesmondhalgh (2015) outlines these difficulties as follows:

- **Media businesses are reliant upon changing audience consumption patterns.** Audience tastes continuously adapt making it incredibly difficult to produce material that guarantees satisfaction.
- **The media industry is reliant on marketing and publicity functions.** Products need the oxygen of publicity if they are to thrive, but controlling the messages delivered by reviewers or publicity partners of other companies is very difficult – even if such organisations are owned by the same parent company as the producer.
- **Media products have limited consumption capacity.** Unlike other businesses, films, television and music-based products tend to be consumed as 'one off' purchases. The 'one off' nature of production means that the huge sums of cash invested to create media products results in a one-time reward.

Hesmondhalgh argues that the risks associated with media creation leads the culture industry to employ a highly tuned range of production and organisational practices. Moreover, because the media industry is sustained, by and large, using the enormous profits achieved from the industry's winners – top grossing films, hit TV dramas and so on – it has to employ an economic model that deliberately overproduces media content.

In short, media companies create as many products as they can in the hope that one or two projects will be hits. By definition, only large-scale companies can successfully engage in this overproduction model given the enormous sums required to finance multiple projects simultaneously and the requisite need to absorb the huge losses of failed products while companies search for big hits.

The ways in which media organisations expand

Hesmondhalgh argues that overproduction has compelled media production companies to expand through mergers or the acquisition of smaller companies. Growth in the media sector has traditionally centred on the following three strategies:

1 **Horizontal integration:** acquiring media companies that operate in similar sectors enables large-scale institutions to achieve scale-based cost savings, while also allowing them to maximise profits by positioning brands so they do not compete with one another. (The benefits of horizontal integration are covered in more detail in Chapter 12.)
2 **Vertical integration:** by acquiring production, distribution and marketing specialist subsidiaries, media conglomerates can control all aspects of their supply chain while also achieving significant cost-saving efficiencies. (Again, a more detailed discussion of the benefits wrought through vertical integration are covered in Chapter 12.)
3 **Multi-sector integration:** buying companies across the culture industry allows for further cross-promotion opportunities and the deployment of brands across media platforms. Most films, for instance, create cross-brand profits through the sale of soundtracks and, in the case of Disney, through their theme park experiences.

Expansion strategies and brand acquisitions

Hesmondhalgh, like Curran and Seaton, is careful to distinguish between those personnel in the media industry who are responsible for producing creative content – the 'symbol creators' as Hesmondhalgh calls them – and those who oversee the wider business-oriented functions of media distribution.

Traditionally, Hesmondhalgh tells us, 'symbol creators are granted considerable autonomy within the process of production – far more, in

---

Box 14.1 Discuss it: what impact does internationalisation have on media?

Hesmondhalgh suggests that media expansion is often pursued so that producers can develop the ability to distribute their products on a global scale (internationalisation). Global distribution, of course, generates the capacity to exponentially increase the profits made from any single investment, but can also result in media products that sacrifice local flavour in order to maximise global appeal.

- In what ways are today's mainstream media products crafted so that they can appeal to international audiences?
- Does today's globalised media landscape mean that we consume a disproportionate number of products that originated in the US? Is this problematic?
- Do audiences suffer when their media stops being local?

---

fact, than most workers in other forms of industry' (Hesmondhalgh, 2015, 32). Writers and directors, journalists and designers, he tells us, are given enough artistic freedom to create products that excite audience engagement. Yet, Hesmondhalgh argues, these loose controls are giving way to tighter business models in which creativity increasingly plays a secondary role to marketing needs and brand development.

This process is evidenced, in part, by the kinds of acquisitions that have dominated media expansion in the past decade. Yes, conglomerates continue to expand both vertically and horizontally, but they are growing in ways that also enable them to acquire lucrative brand-driven content. Disney's $71 billion takeover of Fox in March 2019, for instance, was pursued, in part, to give Disney exclusive access to the hugely successful film and television brands cultivated by 21st Century Fox. And, as a consequence of that acquisition, the task of Disney's creative team in the coming years is not to produce new content, but to maximise the storytelling opportunities that are presented through Disney's ownership of the *X-Men* franchise, *The Simpsons*, *Deadpool* and *Kingsman*.

'The increasing presence and status of marketing,' Hesmondhalgh argues, 'represents a shift in the relations between creativity and commerce' (Hesmondhalgh, 2015, 243). Product-branding decisions, for instance, are increasingly channelled by audience research and focus groups. Product content, too, is pushed in directions that audience data suggests will generate the most sales, while consumption of products using digital platforms has enabled media makers to mine audience data in new and extraordinary ways. Netflix, for example, understands in microscopic detail the consumption patterns of its subscribers, gathering data about what audiences are watching, for how long and for how many episodes. This advanced data harvesting informs Netflix's decisions about what it will commission or indeed who it will commission to make future programming.

Product formatting and risk reduction

Media makers, Hesmondhalgh also tells us, control commercial risks through the careful supervision of distribution and promotion practices, effecting what he calls 'artificial scarcity' – restricting access to products by limiting their availability to platforms that are owned by the parent company of the product (Hesmondhalgh, 2015, 31). Disney, for example, restricts access to its film back catalogue to its vertically integrated distribution services (principally its cable broadcasting infrastructure and Disney+ streaming service). This allows Disney to preserve the mystique of its classic films while also preventing competing broadcasters from using Disney content as a means to grow their own audiences.

Hesmondhalgh, too, draws our attention to the following formatting strategies used by the media industry:

- **Star formatting.** It takes, Hesmondhalgh suggests, 'considerable marketing efforts, in order to break a writer or performer as a new star' (Hesmondhalgh, 2015, 31). Yet star power, once enabled, can deliver ready-made audiences for products.
- **Genre-based formatting.** Labelling media content using genre-based categories allows audiences to identify the potential rewards of consuming a particular media product in advance of consumption. In this sense, genres, Hesmondhalgh argues, operate in the same way that brands pre-promise consumer satisfaction.
- **Serialisation.** The use of sequels and prequels are well-established techniques that are deployed to maximise audience engagement and to allow producers to maximise their investments in serialised material (spin-offs, sequels, etc.). Serialised media needs less investment in marketing activities to create audience visibility. Prequels,

Box 14.2 Apply it: how do film marketing products use established formatting techniques to reduce risk?

Hesmondhalgh's approach can be applied to questions that ask you to consider how products are styled or formatted in order to create audience interest. Use the following questions to help you construct Hesmondhalgh-oriented analysis:

- **Star power:** In what ways does the product use star power? For what is the star best known and for what sorts of audience will the star create appeal? Remember that stars can include writers, directors and journalists as well as performance-oriented stars.

- **Genre-based formatting:** What genre does the product invoke through marketing decisions? How is the product stylised to make its genre explicitly visible? What narrative satisfactions does genre formatting convey to the product's target audience?

- **Remakes and serialisation:** Does the product piggyback on previously successful products? How does it invoke product nostalgia to recapture existing audience interest? In what ways is the product reshaped for a new audience?

- **Independent stylising:** Does the product deliberately invoke a non-mainstream aesthetic? For whom does this create appeal?

Exemplar: *Black Panther* (Eduqas). Hesmondhalgh's assertion that media creativity is subservient to the business and marketing function of the industry is readily visible in *Black Panther*. The movie's use of a predominantly black cast initially looked like a high risk strategy in terms of delivering a mainstream audience, yet the use of the Kendrick Lamar soundtrack and the selection of Michael B. Jordan (*Creed*) as a frontline presence helped secure recognisable star power. The further choice of Martin Freeman (*The Hobbit* and *The Office*) as Everett K. Ross also helped deliver wider European and UK audience appeal. Interestingly, Freeman is the first character we see in the UK general release trailer. Hesmondhalgh would similarly draw attention to the heavy presence of Marvel Studio branding within the trailer and the repetition of the hugely successful and in vogue Superhero formula as a means of reducing the commercial risk through product serialisation.

Further exemplars for set texts from all exam boards are available online at www.essentialmediatheory.com

too, piggyback on pre-existing audience successes, while also enabling institutions to nurture star power through the introduction of new talent within an established, and relatively risk free, formula.

• **Remakes.** The media industry further reduces risk by recycling archived material that has enjoyed prior success. Retellings often seek to recapture audience engagement through nostalgia-based appeals, while also rebranding content so that it fits the needs of a contemporary audience.

• **Independent labelling.** Hesmondhalgh points, too, to the use of 'independents' to produce and market media goods. Independents, he argues, provide a useful means of engaging audiences that are reluctant to consume mainstream media. Conglomerates also delegate production to independents to shield themselves from the impact of content failure on their brand identity. Companies that are truly independent, of course, use their non-mainstream status as a marketing tool, deliberately stylising and formatting their products in ways that make them look and feel alternative.

Concept 2: the effects of the internet revolution are difficult to diagnose

A great deal of academic writing that has tried to diagnose the impact of technological innovation has, Hesmondhalgh argues, done so using overly simplistic formulas. The reality of the digital revolution, he suggests – if it can be described as a revolution at all – is highly complex. More importantly, Hesmondhalgh tells us, the various practices that are seen to constitute 'Web 2.0' represent, in reality, a continuation of the activities of traditional mass media provision.

The faux benefits of cyberspace

Hesmondhalgh suggests that the often cited positive effects of the digital revolution stem from an overly romanticised view of technology as an anti-authoritarian counterweight to traditional power sources. In contrast, he argues that the internet's 'many minor forms of subversion, insubordination and skepticism don't cancel out the enormous concentrations of power in the cultural industries' and further diagnoses those subversive effects as 'representing a disturbance' (Hesmondhalgh, 2015, 361). Hesmondhalgh's relegation of the digital revolution to the status of a mere 'disturbance' centres on a critique of the following two claims regarding technological innovation:

1   That the digital revolution gives power to audiences by enabling cultural participation and that audience control is enabled through feedback mechanisms.

2   That the digital revolution has weakened the power of the mass media.

In many ways, the benefits outlined above are very similar to the 'participatory culture' and 'end of audience' arguments presented, respectively, by Henry Jenkins (Chapter 18) and Clay Shirky (Chapter 19). Hesmondhalgh offers the following three criticisms:

1   **The web gives unequal user access and depends on user skill levels.** When we refer to the internet, we are really describing its capacity to provide a host of benefits, including email functionality, social networking, data storage, entertainment provision, etc. Hesmondhalgh argues that users mostly access internet services in a relatively simplistic manner and usually for information retrieval purposes only – reading online news, browsing the weather and so on. Only a relatively small number of advanced users deploy, or have the skills to deploy, the 'participatory culture' skills that Shirky and Jenkins celebrate.

2   **The internet is dominated by a relatively small number of providers.** Hesmondhalgh points to the dominance of search engines and their ability to point users to a small number of sources. In this sense, the near monopoly of Google as the world's search engine flatly contradicts the notion that the internet has eroded media concentration.

3   **The internet is increasingly dominated by commercialised activity.** Hesmondhalgh argues that the democratising impact of the internet has been further damaged by the adoption of an internet model that relies on advertising revenue. 'Much web content,' Hesmondhalgh argues, 'is permeated by advertising to the extent that it is sometimes difficult to tell where the advertisements end and the content begins' (Hesmondhalgh, 2015, 331). Thus, the neutrality of the information provided by the internet is compromised by commercial imperatives.

Hesmondhalgh, too, suggests that the various forms of technological advances of the digital era are often packaged together in ways that suggest the digital revolution is a singular force. In reality, he argues, technological advances have had varied effects on media forms. Hesmondhalgh identities the following sector specific trends:

- **Digital games.** Despite technological advances, the games sector is still dominated by an oligarch of hardware companies (Sony, Nintendo and Microsoft). Smaller independent production has grown, but those companies are largely responsible for software development (with the exception of Electronic Arts). As a result, Hesmondhalgh suggests, the digital revolution has not really had an effect on the games sector – larger companies are still able to forge cross-media synergies with the film and music sectors, while formatted franchises (*Call of Duty*, *Assassin's Creed*, etc.) are used to maximise audiences and reduce risk.
- **Newspaper industry.** Hesmondhalgh suggests that technological developments have had a significantly adverse impact in this sector. Online media has eroded readerships and forced newspapers to adopt free-to-view online models. Some titles have tried to mitigate the effects of plummeting advertising revenues by implementing pay-per-view firewalls (The *Times*), while other publications such as *The Guardian* have turned to supplementary activities – using their brand recognition to sell dating services, books, holidays, music and other add-ons.
- **Television.** Hesmondhalgh points to the hybridisation of television and the internet to produce on-demand services and to enable time-shifted consumption patterns; however, he also argues that television viewing figures have not reduced greatly. The winners of the analogue to digital broadcast migration, he argues, are more likely to be the small number of global organisations that own the archives of content needed to fill on-demand services. Disney's new global streaming service, Disney+, is a case in point here. Hesmondhalgh, too, points to the continued use of celebrity power to attract audiences to streamed television products, with remakes and serialised content dominating the schedules of on-demand television services.

Box 14.3 Discuss it: what is the real impact of the so-called 'digital revolution'?

- Do you think that modern audiences fluently engage in participatory culture?
- Is participatory culture more likely to be used by a limited number of social groups? Think here in terms of age, gender and class.
- Which groups are likely to be excluded from the benefits of participatory culture?
- Are audiences still passive consumers?

Box 14.4 Apply it: assessing the revolutionary impact of digital innovation on your set texts

Hesmondhalgh's diagnosis of the digital revolution as a 'disturbance' can be integrated in exam responses that ask you to consider the way that digital consumption has impacted on audiences. Discussion that centres around the following three criticisms could be applied to these questions:

1   Digital products continue to engage passive viewing responses.
2   Digital products tend to be made by a relatively small number of providers.
3   The commercialisation of the web weakens the suggestion that the web is a democratising medium.

Exemplar: *Minecraft* (OCR). Jenkins (see Chapter 18) would revel in the way that *Minecraft* audiences have harnessed digital communications technology to effect digital fan power and moreover, in the capacity of those fan groups to engage in 'transmedia learning'. Yet, Hesmondhalgh reminds us, we have to be careful not to over-endorse the impact of digital technologies. The *Minecraft* experience might produce some connected fan activity, yet for every skilled player who is uploading content to the *Minecraft Realm* there are a far greater number of less skilled users who effect traditionally passive engagements. Moreover, the acquisition of *Minecraft* by Microsoft points to the continued presence and power of mass media conglomerates in the gaming industry. *Minecraft* might appear to evidence the democratising effects of the media, but it also provides ample evidence of the way that digital technologies have been co-opted by traditional media practices.

Further exemplars for set texts from all exam boards are available online at www.essentialmediatheory.com

Table 14.1 Speak David Hesmondhalgh

Creative business managers	Those workers who look after the marketing, distribution and financing of media products.
Creative symbol makers	Hesmondhalgh suggests that those workers who create media products (scriptwriters, directors, etc.) are the media's creative symbol makers. Traditionally, creatives were given lots of freedom in the media industry, but, Hesmondhalgh argues, creative decision making is increasingly sidelined in favour of a business-oriented approach.
Genre formatting	Promoting products using genre formatting helps audiences to understand the narrative satisfactions that a product can offer prior to consumption.
Internationalisation	Internationalisation refers to strategies adopted by media makers to maximise their profits and audience reach using global distribution.
Serialisation	Serialisation enables producers to reduce risk by constructing products that have an established audience.
Star formatting	The foregrounding of star power (writers, actors, directors and journalists) in products and promotional material to generate audience interest.

Table 14.2 Hesmondhalgh: ten minute revision

Concept 1: *maximising profits and minimising risks*
- The media industry is prone to risk as a result of shifting audience tastes.
- The media industry tries to reduce risk through overproduction.
- Overproduction strategies, generally speaking, can only be engaged by large media conglomerates.
- Media conglomerates have expanded to enable them to cope with risk.
- Media products are carefully formatted using a number of industry specific strategies to reduce risk.

Concept 2: *the effects of the internet revolution are difficult to diagnose*
- The democratising effects of the digital revolution have been over-exaggerated by some academics.
- Digital media is used by audiences in radically different ways, while only a few users have the necessary skills to engage in participatory culture.
- The internet is dominated by a handful of very powerful companies.
- The commercialisation of the web has further reduced its democratising capacity.

Two theorists who might challenge Hesmondhalgh's thinking
- **Henry Jenkins:** emphasises the positive effects of the digital revolution – suggesting that digital media cultivates online communities and allows audiences to express themselves in positive and creative ways through fan engagement.
- **Clay Shirky:** might argue that large-scale media providers will be replaced by products that are created by everyday users, or that mass media content will be significantly controlled by audience feedback mechanisms.

---

15 Media modelling effects

Albert Bandura

The exploration of aggression had been a point of interest for psychologists and philosophers long before Bandura introduced the world to his Bobo doll experiments. Sigmund Freud, for example, explained the origins of aggression as an innate and instinctive emotional response. Excessive masculine aggression, he reasoned, was present as a result of the male sex drive, suggesting that male aggression is driven by a latent fear of castration by our fathers.

Post-war psychologists, too, looked inwards to explain the presence of aggression – some connecting outwardly violent behaviour to the genetic disposition of individuals or to hormonal imbalances. Even as late as 1965, the psychologist P.A. Jacobs argued that a disproportionate number of institutionalised men, those committed to prison or mental institutions, were born with an extra chromosome that produced hyper-masculine behaviours. Aggression, Jacobs reasoned, was genetic or the product of innate dispositions that were beyond the control of the individual.

Bandura's experiments, however, led him to a remarkably different set of conclusions and gave birth to a psychological school of thought that was later labelled 'social learning theory'. Bandura's research, in short, suggested that our behaviours are not governed by innate traits or genetic impulses but that our environments – the human environment in particular – shapes the way we behave.

Concept 1: violent behaviours are learned through modelling

Bandura's psychological experiments led him to conclude that behaviours are acquired as a result of the following two processes:

1   **Direct experience.** Individuals, Bandura argued, learn or replicate aggressive acts as a result of their experiences of aggression.
Children might learn to be aggressive from the models of negative
behaviour that parents provide, or, conversely, they might reject
violent behaviours as a result of parent-induced punishments and
sanctions.

2   **Modelled learning.** Bandura intuited that direct experience
alone could not account for all of our human traits. Individuals, he
hypothesised, could not possibly have witnessed enough directly
modelled behaviour to account for the complexity of their own
behaviour. Behaviours, Bandura conjectured, must therefore be
learned by watching the actions of others – through what he called
'vicarious learning'. For example, a child who witnesses the
violent behaviour of a classmate might later imitate the actions he
or she sees. Conversely, if a child witnesses the same behaviour
being punished, they might be more likely to be inhibited from
copying those actions. 'It is evident,' Bandura writes, 'that human
behaviour is to a large extent socially transmitted, either deliberately or inadvertently' (Bandura, 1973, 68).

Concept 2: audiences copy media modelling

Bobo dolls and symbolic modelling

Bandura's initial research, in the 1960s, was conducted using nursery
aged children who were made to watch a variety of adult role models
execute a series of aggressive acts on an inflatable Bobo doll. The
experiments were designed to investigate whether the children would

---

**Box 15.1 Think about it: from where have you learned
your own behaviours?**

- What influence have your parents had on your behaviours? In
  what ways have their expectations affected your outlook?
- Have your friends ever affected your behaviour in a negative or
  positive way?
- In what ways did the rules and expectations of your primary and
  secondary schools shape your behaviour?

copy the adults' actions when left alone, and, overwhelmingly, the observations that Bandura's team noted from the experiment were that the children did replicate the aggressive behaviours they had witnessed. Aggressive behaviours, Bandura concluded, were most certainly learned through direct modelling.

But what shocked the Bobo doll research team the most was the response of the children when they replaced the adult role models with filmed sequences that depicted the same aggressive behaviour. To their surprise, the children responded in a similarly violent manner, leading Bandura to conclude that behaviours can be transmitted through the representational effects of television.

Bandura's conclusions regarding media viewing, moreover, suggested that media-based representations of violence might indeed have a more concentrated effect than direct modelling. He drew attention to the following three factors that amplify the effects of television consumption on behavioural modelling:

- **Attentional processes.** The effectiveness of a modelled behaviour is dependent on the degree to which the observer's attention is focused on the behaviour being modelled. In the real world, he argued, our attention is less focused on modelled action than when we watch television. 'Indeed, models presented in televised form are so effective in holding attention,' Bandura writes, 'that viewers learn the depicted behavior regardless of whether or not they are given extra incentives to do so' (Bandura, 1973, 70).
- **Role models and social learning.** The effectiveness of modelling is also swayed by the people we are watching. If behaviour is

---

Box 15.2 Discuss it: how did the media affect you?

- In what ways did watching television affect your behaviour as a young child? Did you or your brothers and sisters copy the negative behaviours you saw on television?
- Did you have any media role models that you wanted to be like when you were younger? What effect did those role models have on your behaviour?
- Is television hypnotic? Does it capture our attention in a way that no other media form can?

modelled by aspirational role models, Bandura argued, we are more likely to want to copy their behaviour. The level of power and prestige of television-oriented role models therefore makes it more likely that they will have a greater impact on audience behaviours.

• **Retention processes.** Representations of behaviours that are visually vivid or symbolically constructed will be retained for longer periods. Given that television and film are encoded in a visually rich manner – through costuming, set or acting styles – the resulting effect, Bandura argued, is much richer than real-life modelling.

Television fiction and the commercialisation of violence

Bandura argued that, problematically, television and film products are rich with violent content, and, as a result, adverse television modelling effects are widespread. Violence is endemic within the media, Bandura argued, because producers, script writers and directors are themselves too desensitised to the effects of screen violence to raise objections to problematic content. Moreover, the media relies on conflict to quickly and effectively engage audience attention, using depictions of violence to produce cheap thrills in stories. Bandura, too, pointed to the incremental concentration of violent content that results from broadcaster competition, arguing that television producers continuously intensify violent content within their products as a means of poaching their competitors' audiences.

Video violence effects

Even though Bandura's work did not directly comment on the capacity of gaming to produce violent behaviours, it is routinely invoked to

---

Box 15.3 Apply it (OCR and AQA): violence in television set texts

Both OCR and AQA suggest that students should be able to apply Bandura to their television set texts. These applications might be prompted by the following question types:

• **OCR style question.** Evaluate the relevance of Bandura's media effects theory in long form television drama. (10 marks)

- **AQA style question.** According to Bandura's media effects theory, television products model behaviours that audiences can copy or emulate and the behaviours they model are often negative. How valid are Bandura's claims concerning audience responses? You should refer to your television set texts to support your answer. (25 marks)

Answers could make reference to the following:

- **Analysis of specific moments within the set texts that offer modelled violence.** What negative behaviours might audiences learn from these moments?
- **Analysis that explores the narrative context of modelled behaviour.** Is the violent behaviour of characters rewarded or punished across story arcs? How might these factors concentrate or inhibit audience responses?
- **Role model effects.** In what ways does star power or the idealised presentation of violent content help concentrate the product's modelling impact?
- **Attentional effects.** Does the way the product is consumed alter any modelling effect it might have? Might on-demand binge watching, for instance, result in an intensified modelling experience?
- **Vivid visual encoding effects.** Is modelled negative behaviour likely to have an effect on the product's audience as a result of a heightened aesthetic presentation?
- **Positive modelling effects.** Does the product have the potential to produce positive learning for the audience? How and where?

Arguments and theories you could also use that suggest audiences do not necessarily engage with products in the way that Bandura suggests:

- **Henry Jenkins:** use Jenkins' ideas concerning fan communities to develop discussion concerning any potential positive effects of set texts. In what ways are fans using set texts to explore positive rather negative aspects of their identity?
- **Stuart Hall:** use Hall's encoding and decoding model to critique Bandura's ideas. Not all audiences respond to products in the same way – we decode texts using our contextual knowledge and experience.

Exemplar responses for set texts from all exam boards are available at www. essentialmediatheory.com

Box 15.4 Apply it (OCR): using Bandura in synoptic set text questions

Opportunities to apply Bandura's theoretical perspective are also available within the synoptic question of the component two exam. You could connect Bandura's arguments to question types in the following ways:

Questions that have a representation focus

•   Representation of violence might be minimised because producers are mindful of modelling effects that products could have on their target audience.

•   Representations of violent content might be deliberately minimised as a result of regulatory codes that explicitly restrict the impact of modelled behaviour on audiences.

Questions that have a language focus

•   Genre-based productions might contain violent content as a core convention or audience expectation.

•   Narratives are conventionally driven by conflict. Conflict inevitably raises issues regarding the effects of violence on audiences in terms of modelling behaviours.

Questions that have an institution focus

•   Commercial organisations, arguably, are more likely to include violence as a means of attracting audiences.

•   Netflix content is not directly subject to UK regulatory codes. Does this make it more likely to produce material that produces modelled violence?

•   On-demand broadcasting cannot reduce the effects of modelled violence through the use of scheduling restrictions or watersheds.

Exemplar responses for set texts from all exam boards are available at www.essentialmediatheory.com

suggest that a link exists between real-life aggression and game playing. American mass shootings by teenagers, for instance, are regularly explained as occurring as a direct result of violent game content. Commentators often draw attention to the following factors in suggesting that a causal link exists between game playing and real-world violence:

- **Attention factors.** Players control and direct gaming avatars to exercise violence meaning that a direct connection exists between player actions and the resulting violent behaviours that are depicted on-screen. This intimate connection is seen to promote violent behaviours in the real world.
- **Players are rewarded for violent actions.** Gaming engines generate scores and rewards for kills, while narrative progression in games is often only revealed once violent episodes are resolved by players. Reward systems of these kinds are seen to promote violent behaviour as a result of positive modelling experiences.
- **Violence is portrayed without moral justification or explanation.** Games often require players to kill innocent bystanders or to inflict violence on defenceless characters. The casual nature of these violent acts, some would suggest, desensitises players to the effects of real-world violence.
- **Video games are immersive.** Players are thought to consume video games in isolation − without the mediating effects of others to help them question their actions.
- **Realistic violence.** Gaming graphics engines are increasingly capable of producing more realistic portrayals, and, in doing so, limit a gamer's ability to distinguish real-world actions from those experienced in gaming narratives.
- **Video games are addictive.** Long periods of gameplay produce sustained negative modelling experiences.

Regulatory frameworks as protection

The Pan European Gaming Information (PEGI) rating system has responded to the concerns surrounding gaming content through the creation of its advisory ratings code. The code principally protects vulnerable players through an age classification system and works to alert parents to the following types of gaming content:

- **Violent content.** Games with lower age ratings must contain minimal violence, and while PEGI 12-rated games are allowed to include violent content it must be presented in a non-realistic manner. Violence perpetrated on innocent characters is only allowed in PEGI 18-rated games.
- **Drugs, alcohol and tobacco use.** Depictions of this nature are limited to PEGI 16-certified games and above, while glamorised

depictions of drug taking are only allowed in PEGI 18-certified games.

- **Discrimination.** Games that contain problematic ethnic, religious, nationalistic or other negative stereotypes are again restricted to a PEGI 18 certificate.

Box 15.5 Discuss it: video game regulation and imitable behaviour

- How effective do you think the PEGI ratings system is in protecting young people from the harmful effects of gaming? How might young people circumvent that system?
- What evidence would you present to critique the view that video games induce violent behaviour?

Box 15.6 Apply it (Eduqas and AQA): using Bandura in video game set text questions

Eduqas and AQA questions that ask you to apply Bandura's ideas to games and online set texts might be styled as follows:

- **Eduqas.** Consider the relationship that exists between video game technologies and the patterns of response they produce in audiences. Answer with reference to your video game set text. (12 marks)
- **AQA.** How convincing are the arguments that video game products produce violent behaviours? In your answer you should refer to your Close Study Products. (20 marks)

Answers to the above could focus on the following key areas:

- **Attention and immersion factors.** Gaming technologies produce narratives that are longer and far more complex than other media forms – potentially leading to a more concentrated modelling effect.
- **Graphic content.** Provide knowledge and analysis of moments in set text gameplay and/or marketing materials where graphic violence is depicted. What potential modelling effects might those moments have on audiences? In what ways do these moments glamorise screen violence?
- **Gameplay that provides rewards for violent actions.** Analyse how your gaming set texts reward audiences for violent play.

Identify the use of violence to: unlock side missions, advance narratives, provide new weapons or to advance online multiplayer rankings. What impact do these reward systems have in promoting violent behaviours?

- **Portrayals of violence that have moral justification or explanation.** Discuss moments in set texts where protagonist violence is disproportionate to antagonist actions. These moments might also be found in marketing materials. Does this sort of game violence desensitise players?
- **Video games are targeted at impressionable teenage audiences.** Video games are regulated, but is PEGI effective in prohibiting under-age game consumption? Discuss the effects of online distribution on teenage consumption and the ease with which young audiences can circumvent age checks.

Exemplar responses for set texts from all exam boards are available at www.essential mediatheory.com

The arguments against negative video game modelling

In 2008, Henry Jenkins famously rallied to the defence of the video games industry, arguing that the panic surrounding gaming violence was founded on some questionable assumptions (Jenkins 2019). He highlights the following factors in defence of video game playing:

- **Studies that link game playing time and criminal behaviours are flawed.** Advocates of the argument that video games produce violent behaviour often point to studies that identify video game use by violent youth offenders as disproportionately widespread. Yet, Jenkins points out, video gaming is so universally practised among teenagers that any concrete cause and effect link is highly tenuous.
- **Game play is not solitary.** Jenkins points to research that suggests most gameplay takes place within a social context, either physically or across a digital network. Researchers point to the potential benefits of communal play, suggesting that players hone communication skills by working together to solve gaming problems.
- **Audiences are able to separate gameplay from real life.** Games might indeed illicit violent responses on-screen, but research suggests that players are able to distinguish screen violence from their real-world activities.

Box 15.7 Apply it: diagnose the positive effects of video game set texts on their audiences

Video games and moral panics

Critics suggest that video game violence concerns are magnified by the media, and that the moral panic concerning the effects of gameplay are symptomatic of society's wider anxieties about the use of new technologies by young people. Think about the following questions to help you diagnose the positive effects of your video game set texts:

- In what ways do your set texts have a positive effect on audiences behaviours?
- Do any of your gaming set texts teach their audiences new skills? How do they do this?

Exemplar responses for set texts from all exam boards are available at www.essentialmediatheory.com

---

Table 15.1 Speak Albert Bandura

Attentional effects	Bandura argues that media products are more likely to produce modelled behaviour because of the focused attention they command while engaging with them.
Desensitisation	Desensitisation normalises violent behaviours as a result of repeated exposure.
Modelled learning	Bandura suggests that we learn new behaviours by watching other people (direct modelling). Behaviours can be inhibited if we see others being punished; conversely, we copy behaviours when they are rewarded.
Representational modelling	The process of watching behaviours on-screen. Bandura concludes that representational modelling can be equally, if not more, powerful than direct modelling.
Role model effects	Bandura argues that watching others we hold in high regard (on-screen stars/heroes) can amplify the impact of any modelled behaviours.

Table 15.2 Bandura: ten minute revision

Concept 1: *violent behaviours are learned through modelling*
- Humans learn much of their behaviour through social interaction.
- Social learning can occur as a result of first-hand experience.
- Social learning can also occur by watching others' experiences.

Concept 2: *audiences can copy media representations of negative behaviour*
- Representational modelling can have a powerful effect on the behaviours of media audiences.
- Modelled behaviours by role models and the vivid visual encoding systems of media products further concentrate the effects of representational modelling.
- Violence is an endemic feature of media content.

Three theorists who might challenge Bandura's thinking
- **Stuart Hall:** would argue that media products do not produce a cause and effect learning response – audiences decode the media they engage with using contextual knowledge.
- **Henry Jenkins:** emphasises the positive effects of media consumption – suggesting that the media forges communities and allows audiences to express themselves in positive and creative ways through fan engagement.
- **George Gerbner:** would argue that the media should not be measured just in terms of its impact on individual learning behaviours but also on the cumulative effects of mass media consumption on wider social attitudes.

---

16 Cultivation theory

George Gerbner

Born in 1919, Gerbner experienced first-hand the growth of mass media, from its early infancy in the 1920s to the television boom of the 1960s and 1970s. It is difficult for contemporary audiences to fully comprehend a world without mass media or to appreciate the impact widespread television ownership produced. For Gerbner, however, that transition was a lived experience, and must have prompted his interest in the effects of mass media consumption on wider society.

Gerbner's research, much like that of his academic contemporary, Bandura, focused on screen depictions of violence and the attitudinal changes that could be induced as a result of watching television conflict. The conclusions that Gerbner formed in response to that research were profound in their suggestion that television viewing could radically change the way we perceive the real world.

Concept 1: fear cultivation

Gerbner argues that media communications, principally television-based media, replaced a set of pre-existing symbol systems that had dominated the cultural and social lives of individuals up until the early twentieth century. Society, Gerbner suggests, uses religious or cultural products to guide the attitudes and behaviours of its constituent members. Those systems, prior to television, were embedded via the church or educational practices. Mass media, Gerbner argues, replaced these 'common symbolic environments' (Gerbner and Morgan, 2016, 193) to become the dominant socialising force of our age.

'Television,' Gerbner tells us, 'is the first centralized cultural influence to permeate both the initial and final years of life – as well as the years in between' (Gerbner and Morgan, 2016, 230). The sheer number of people who were watching television in the 1960s led Gerbner to hypothesise that the mass media produced a broad enculturation effect, transmitting ideas and attitudes on a scale that had not been witnessed before. The power of television, Gerbner claims, is not narrowly defined as something that can impact on the behaviours of a few solitary individuals in society (as Bandura suggests): television, he argues, influences all sections of society and is capable of inducing attitudinal change across our entire social network.

Gerbner isolates the following factors that invest television with a capacity to effect widescale social change:

- **Television is easily decodable.** You do not need to read or be literate to understand television. The meaning of programme content is readily consumed by everyone, from pre-school infants to the elderly.
- **Television access is largely cost free.** Unlike other cultural products – the theatre, cinema and books – television consumption is relatively inexpensive and, as a result, is readily consumed across all sections of society, by both rich and poor alike.
- **Television consumption is intensified.** Time spent watching television far outweighs comparable cultural activities such as church going or reading, amplifying further the effect of televisual messages.
- **Television is a centralised and homogenous producer of cultural symbols.** The centralised nature of television production means that cultural messages are controlled by a handful of media makers.
- **Television products are encoded using realism.** Television drama, Gerbner suggests, is so reflective of the real world that it is difficult for us to understand that fictional products are not constructed versions of reality. 'How many of us have ever been in an operating room, a criminal courtroom, a police station or jail, or corporate boardroom, or a movie studio?,' Gerbner asks, 'how much of our real world has been learned from fictional worlds?' (Gerbner and Morgan, 2016, 232).

Box 16.1 Discuss it: how does television impact our view of the world?

- How much time do you spend watching television? How much time do your parents or guardians spend watching TV?
- How much of your understanding of the real world is constructed through television?
- What effects does watching television have on society?
- Do you think Gerbner's arguments regarding the impact of television on social attitudes is just as valid in today's digital world? Why or why not?

The Violence Index

Gerbner's realisation that television could be having a profound effect on the collective consciousness of society led him to set up the Cultural Indicators project in 1969 to measure the levels of violence across programming. Gerbner was interested in confirming exactly how much television content was driven by sequences that depicted symbolic aggression. Violence, Gerbner hypothesised, was a cheap mechanism that producers used to capture audience interest or to elicit easy emotional responses. Violence, he argued, had thus become an endemic feature of both drama and factual television, and was, he further hypothesised, subtly affecting the attitudes of mass audiences.

The project's findings, dubbed the 'Violence Index' by Gerbner, revealed that depictions of on-screen conflict within mainstream US television were widespread. Key findings recorded at end of the project's 9-year tracking period in 1975 included:

- 8 of every 10 programmes across all networks contained some element of violence.
- More alarmingly, 9 out of 10 children's programmes at weekends contained violent content.
- The average number of violent episodes across programming per hour was 8 – rising to 16 per hour for children's programming.

Gerbner also indexed the following trends regarding character involvement in violence:

- Females were consistently depicted as more vulnerable than men, with 1.32 female victims recorded for each episode of violence as opposed to an average rate of 1.19 male victims per episode.
- Elderly women, single and non-white females were especially prone to victimisation with white males found to be the least likely victims of violent acts.
- The victimisation of powerless female characters was a staple starter in a significant number of drama shows.

The issue of violent content was not just confined to television drama. Gerbner suggested that news-based media was equally problematic; this, in part, is because of the high volume of time it occupies in broadcasters' schedules, while the selective processes of news presentation pushes the most violent events to the fore. 'If it bleeds, it leads', is the old media adage.

The effect of factual programming offers further significance in that viewers inherently understand drama-based violence to be fictitious at some level. Representations of real-world violence, however, have the capacity to convey a more profound attitudinal audience-based response. If we watch lots of media content that paints the real world as violent or aggressive, then, perhaps, we are more likely to believe that it actually is.

Box 16.2 Apply it: how violent are your set texts?

- Which of your set texts contain moments of violence? Look especially at TV and video game set texts.
- Which set texts contain the most numerous or significant moments of violence?
- Who are the victims and perpetrators of violence in your set texts? Are there any problematic trends? Are more women, non-white ethnicities or older people constructed as victims?
- What evidence could you present to suggest that news-oriented set texts are just as problematic as drama-based media forms in terms of the amount of violent content they report?
- Gerbner's Violence Index researchers included comic violence, accidents and natural disasters in their tallies. Is this problematic?

Examples of analysis that applies Gerbner's ideas to set texts from a range of exam boards are available at www.essentialmediatheory.com

Cultivating fear and danger

The Cultural Indicators project was designed to place pressure on American television networks to reduce violent content; it succeeded, for a while at least, with a number of US networks pulling graphic depictions from many prime time shows. But Gerbner was also interested in measuring the way endemic television violence shifted the attitudes and outlooks of American audiences and devised a series of follow-up studies that compared the real-world perspectives of 'heavy viewers' with those who were less exposed to violent television content.

Gerbner's research conclusively established what he called a 'cultivation differential' – those audiences that were exposed to more television content had a heightened perception of real-world violence. Heavy viewing not only made people less trustful of others, but also significantly increased their fear of becoming a real-world crime victim. Gerbner identified the following viewing effects:

- **Resonance:** He found that people who lived in high crime areas and who were heavy television viewers were subject to a double-dose effect. He concluded that for those who had experience of crime, television viewing significantly amplified their fear of real-world crime.

- **Mainstreaming:** He also concluded that heavy viewers who were significantly less informed about real-life crime – perhaps as a result of living in a safe neighbourhood – also reported significantly increased perceptions of violence in the real world. He thus concluded that watching television could lead to attitudinal change irrespective of whether viewers had any objective evidence to corroborate what they were seeing on-screen in the real world.

Both mainstreaming and resonance suggest that heavy mass media consumption – no matter the extent of real-world experiences – made viewers susceptible to the messages of media products. Long-term exposure to media violence, Gerbner suggested, resulted in viewers adopting 'mean world syndrome'. Television, he concluded, convinces its audiences that society is far more dangerous and violent than it actually is.

Box 16.3 Discuss it: how violent do you think the real world is?

- What effects does news reportage have on the public's perception of crime? Can you evidence media content that has potentially cultivated public fear?
- Do any of your friends or family members have an over-exaggerated fear of crime as a result of media consumption?
- Is the fear of a particular crime exaggerated by news reporting? For example, knife crime or burglary?
- In what ways does the public's perception of crime affect the way we treat criminals?

Concept 2: media consumption leads audiences to accept mainstream ideologies

Violence on television represents symbolic power

Television news and drama does not merely present viewers with portrayals of violence; it parades before them a steady stream of victims and victimisers. Television creates winners and losers. It organises social groups hierarchically by telling us who is most likely to die or be shot. Media violence, moreover, suggests who we ought to control and who we should trust to do the controlling. Gerbner draws our attention to the following symbolic effects that are created as a result of on-screen violence:

- **Media violence defines powerless characters.** The over-representation of key groups in victim counts – women, non-whites, the elderly – is a symbolic demonstration, Gerbner argues, of their ideologically inferior status in the real world.
- **Media violence defines powerful characters.** The dominance of white males as heroic law-makers or law enforcers simultaneously suggests their superior social position.
- **Narrative conventions reinforce authority.** The lack of tragic narratives and the dominance of happy endings in television drama construct a clear-cut ideological message. There may be bad people in the world, but the law and authority will always win through. The good guys never die, of course.

- **News reportage stigmatises key groups.** Media narratives help to justify the use of violence against key groups – terrorists, protestors, criminals – and play a symbolic role in reinforcing existing sources of authority.

- **Audience protest is subjugated.** Because viewers interpret the world as mean, Gerbner suggests, they come to overly rely on established authority sources for protection. Thus, audiences are passive when confronted with real-world authorities or, likewise, their view of authority as all powerful (as represented by the media) makes them too afraid to take a stand against any perceived injustice.

Constructing content for the mainstream

Gerbner also takes aim at the financial imperatives that drive commercial television. Much like Curran and Seaton, he critiques the media's reliance on advertising revenue, arguing that commercial media forms need to develop mass audiences to sustain advertising income and, as a result, the media frames political debates and current affairs in ways that neutralise controversy.

'Competition for the largest possible audience,' Gerbner argues, 'means striving for the broadest and most conventional appeals, blurring sharp conflicts, blending and balancing competing perspectives' (Gerbner and Morgan, 2016, 308). Thus, mainstream media broadcasters sanitise alternative viewpoints by purposefully adopting a bland middle-of-the road perspective. This position means that they avoid offending or alienating mainstream audiences and the respective advertising clientele they attract, and on whom broadcasters are financially dependent.

Cultivation theory: magazines and the internet

Gerbner's interest in television violence was prompted by the radical expansion of television ownership during the post-war years. And although his research focused on the widespread effects of violence, he hypothesised that television could also be responsible for the enculturation of a range of other attitudinal changes and acknowledged that other mass media forms were capable of similar widespread effects.

The academic Jonathan Bignell took up Gerbner's cue, applying a cultivation theory perspective to analyse the effects of magazines on

---

Box 16.4 Discuss it: does contemporary commercial media reinforce mainstream beliefs?

Mainstreaming effects in newspapers

- In what ways do the newspapers you have studied present ideas in a middle-of-the-road manner?
- What evidence could you present to suggest that the mainstream media deliberately avoids radical discussion so that both mainstream audiences and advertising revenues are maintained?

Mainstreaming effects of the internet

- In what ways has the introduction of advertising effected YouTube content? Has advertising sanitised vlogging?

Mainstreaming effects of television

- Do streaming providers (Netflix/Amazon) take more risks than commercial broadcasters? What are those risks? Where are they evidenced?
- In what ways could we challenge Gerbner's idea that television constructs middle-of-the-road programming? Are modern audiences more tolerant of radical content?

---

readers, concluding, as a result, that lifestyle-oriented publications construct a fictional version of gender that readers apply to their real-world selves. 'By constructing a mythic community for men or women,' Bignell writes, 'magazines delineate the social meaning of gender' (Bignell, 2002, 77). Magazines, he concludes, enculture far-reaching beauty ideals that profoundly shape the way that men and women think about themselves and each other.

Likewise, much commentary has been expended on the real-world effects of social media and the capacity for our increasingly divisive digital conversations to translate into real-world aggression. *The Observer* journalist Mark Townsend, for example, draws attention to the growth of right-wing extremism on online social media and the potential that such content has to radicalise audiences. 'An indicator of the evolving challenge,' he writes, 'is the recent move by MI5 to wrest control from the police of investigations into far-right plots'

Townsend confirms, more worryingly, that, 'Four extreme rightwing terror plots were foiled in the year to June 2018, fuelling disquiet over online forums and their ability to disseminate extremist ideology' (Townsend, 2019). Gerbner might have formed his conclusions some 50 years ago, but his ideas are readily applicable to the mass media of today.

Figure 16.1 The Daily Mirror front page (12 December 2018).
© Mirrorpix.

Box 16.5 Apply it: use cultivation theory to create exam responses for audience-based questions

Gerbner's cultivation theory can provide a useful starting point for exam questions that ask you to consider how audiences might respond to set texts or unseen products. Think about these questions to help construct exam relevant analysis:

- What kinds of fears does the media product produce?
- In what ways could the text amplify an audience's existing fears?
- How might the text produce new attitudes through mainstreaming effects?
- In what ways does the product convey symbolic power?
- Does the product present middle-of-the-road reportage to preserve its commercial integrity?

Exemplar – The *Daily Mirror*: 'Children of 11 Selling Zombie Drugs' (Eduqas).

The *Daily Mirror* front page (see Figure 16.1) provides an excellent example of a media product that contributes, in Gerbner's view, to 'mean world syndrome'. The article constructs a heightened awareness of criminal activity through the use of a horror-oriented semantic field ('zombie', 'evil') and also through hyperbole ('epidemic'). Gerbner would argue that audiences that have experience of real-world crime would respond to the article via a 'resonance'-oriented effect – the front page amplifying their pre-existing perceptions and fears of drug-related crime – while audiences whose real-world experiences are largely crime free would similarly respond (albeit to a lesser degree) through a mainstreaming effect. The article, Gerbner might also argue, produces a stigmatisation of illegal activity, positioning the audience to develop a broad submissive acceptance of authority as a result of their exaggerated perceptions of law enforcement activities in the UK. This kind of media, Gerbner contentiously suggests, does not perform a social benefit; rather, it constrains its readership, paralysing them with fear and unwittingly inducing social obedience.

Further exemplars for set texts from all exam boards are available online at www.essentialmediatheory.com

---

Box 16.6 Compare it: using Stuart Hall's reception theory as a contrast to Gerbner

Stuart Hall's reception theory model can be used to provide a contrasting perspective to Gerbner's cultivation theory. While Gerbner's analysis suggests that audiences have no choice in submitting to media effects, Hall, in contrast, argues that we can construct oppositional decodings of texts as a result of our contextual positions (see Chapter 17).

Table 16.1 Speak George Gerbner

Enculturation	The process of learning social norms or behaviours through watching others or by engaging with culture. The media contributes to the enculturation of individuals by making them adopt specific attitudes or outlooks.
Homogenised cultural effects	Television has a homogeneous cultural effect in that its reach and lack of content diversity makes us think the same things or adopt the same attitudes.
Mainstreaming	Gerbner suggests that some groups are less likely to be affected by television (more educated audiences or those who have not experienced violence in real life, for instance). Although the attitudes of these groups are affected to a lesser extent by the media, they are still prone to some attitudinal shift as a result of consumption. Television can, therefore, cultivate problematic attitudes and beliefs within mainstream society where they had not existed before.
Mean world syndrome	An outlook that considers the world to be far more violent or selfish than it really is.
Middle-of-the-road reportage	The use of balanced reporting to foster large-scale audiences and boost advertising revenue. Middle-of-the-road reportage positions new or radical ideas as dangerous, subtly enforcing existing power structures.
Resonance	The process of amplifying an idea, attitude or belief already held by audiences through media consumption.
Stigmatisation	The process of demonising groups, individuals or ideas through media representations.
Symbolic power	Those who have power in media narratives (in terms of gender, class, ethnicity) are legitimised as real-world power sources.

Table 16.2 Gerbner: ten minute revision

Concept 1: *media products shape attitudes and perceptions of the world at large*
- Storytelling performs an enculturation role helping to shape our attitudes and social values.
- Mass media has replaced other institutions, most notably religion and education, as the principle constructor of symbolic storytelling.
- Television has had a homogenising effect on society – we all watch or engage in the same symbolic stories as a result of mass media.
- Television schedules are saturated with violent content that cultivates a widespread fear in society – 'mean world syndrome'.
- The media can produce resonance or mainstreaming effects on audiences.

Concept 2: *media consumption leads audiences to accept established power structures and mainstream ideologies*
- Mass media narratives create symbolic representations of power that affect our real-world view.
- Mass media products over-exaggerate the power and scope of real-world authorities.
- Mass media products marginalise alternative viewpoints as a result of middle-of-the-road reportage.

Three theorists who challenge Gerbner's thinking
- **Stuart Hall:** would argue that media products do not produce a cause and effect response – audiences decode the media using contextual knowledge.
- **Henry Jenkins:** emphasises the positive effects of media consumption – suggesting that the media forges communities and allows audiences to express themselves in positive and creative ways through fan engagement.
- **Albert Bandura:** would argue that the media directly impacts an individual's behaviour and induces consumers to be violent. Gerbner, in contrast, suggests that media consumption prompts an attitudinal rather than a behavioural response.

---

17 Reception theory

Stuart Hall

Stuart Hall's 1973 essay, 'Encoding/Decoding', was groundbreaking. Prior to Hall's work, communications models defined the process of media consumption in a relatively straightforward manner, suggesting that the media constructed messages that audiences readily consumed without question. The media was thought to inject ideas into audiences, who offered, in return, little resistance to what they saw, read or heard. Hall suggested otherwise, asserting that media consumers were alert and critical readers, listeners and viewers.

Stuart Hall's writing perhaps captures the spirit of the era and the numerous possibilities that were unfolding for audiences during the 1970s – to explore alternative viewpoints and to challenge the mainstream ideologies of the post-war years. Certainly, Hall, as a Jamaican immigrant, understood what it meant to stand outside of the mainstream, and he was critically aware of the way culture could be used to establish and maintain social inequalities. The revolutionary impact of his media writing, however, cannot be understated. Hall reframed the 'cause and effect' consumption models of the 1950s and 1960s, acknowledging for the first time the theoretical possibility that audiences do not engage with media products as passive recipients but as critically engaged readers of media texts.

Concept 1: encoding and decoding

Encoding produces a mediated view of the world

In Hall's reception theory formula, media products are encoded using established production processes. A newspaper does not simply record events as they happen. Stories are harvested by experienced reporters.

Events are framed using established story structures. Editorial biases shape stories to construct versions of the truth that are entertaining, marketable or persuasive.

Encoding processes, therefore, will always construct a mediated world view. Journalists do not just report the raw facts; they present a carefully orchestrated version of those events. They carefully select interviewees who are chosen to convey a specific outlook. Footage is sequenced, with key imagery chosen to underline, question or justify those viewpoints.

Hall further suggests that media encoding processes are framed using a variety of formal codes, both visual and aural. These codes might not necessarily be connected to the stories reported, but they enhance the messages that are relayed. The visual look and colour coding of the television news studio, for example, gives weight and authority to the broadcaster's messages. The formal attire of newsreaders similarly conveys their professionalism, while the drum-laden intros of news bulletins are designed to imply gravity and impending seriousness. It is no accident that the BBC allows us to look beyond the presenter and see the vast newsroom with its army of journalists working in the background. The formal codes of news are thus weighted to convince us that news narratives have been carefully researched by a team of diligent and experienced professionals.

Encoding and the production process

Hall draws our attention to the following production factors that channel media encoding:

- **Routines of production:** the way that products are made and the routines followed channel encoding effects. The 24-hour news cycle prompts newspapers to favour breaking news at the expense of older stories, while the use of courtroom reportage as a routine journalistic activity inevitably means that criminal cases feature heavily in news coverage. Processes govern meaning, and an understanding of how the media is made helps us detect the hidden biases that media products relay to their audiences.
- **Genre-driven mediation:** genre-driven rules often frame the visual or narrative structures of media products. In news reportage, for example, stories are often constructed in a highly formulaic way, recycling familiar themes, events and characters in genre-driven

rituals. Hall was particularly interested, for instance, in the way that newspapers demonised black masculinity in the 1970s and 1980s, and the almost endemic use of the black male mugger stereotype within reportage. We might argue that those same stereotypes have resurfaced in the contemporary media's coverage of the UK knife crime epidemic. In fictional products, too, the narrative structure and character expectations of genres routinely encode specific representations within products. In crime drama, writers continue to manufacture female victims and lone wolf masculine villains – genre-encoding rules presiding over any wider gender-based concerns.

* **Institutional context:** the media, Hall reminds us, is constructed by fixed networks of people who collectively create a select perspective. The views of those networks might lead to political bias – indeed, media producers might deliberately choose to employ people who share the same political bias.

* **Predictions regarding audience taste:** media producers encode products in ways they think will appeal to their audience. Assumptions regarding audience tastes are used to make sure that products are commercially viable, yet the extent to which products predict or, indeed, infer audience thinking is highly debatable. Media producers may, in fact, be constructing rather than reflecting audience attitudes as a result of these practices.

Decoding

Hall suggests that media encoding provides us with an entry point to understanding the effects that products have on their audiences. An understanding that just explores encoding, however, does not fully detail the process through which the media creates meaning. Products may encode meanings, Hall argues, but that does not necessarily suggest that audiences understand or decode those ideas in the same way.

Media decoding, Hall argues, is not straightforward. Media products, he suggests, produce a variety of audience-based readings because the media is predominantly constructed using visual signs. These signs, he further suggests, create an iconic/connotative effect rather than an explicit/denotative exposition. When we see an image of a cow, for example, we can all recognise and name the animal appropriately, but we do not arrive at the same conclusions regarding the image's connotative meaning. Some readers might associate cows with nature or regard them as a symbol that represents the English countryside. Conversely, vegans or

> ## Box 17.1 Think about it: what is more important – encoding or decoding?
>
> - Do you think that media encoding or decoding is more important in terms of the overriding effect of a media product?
> - Are media products polysemic? What arguments might you present to suggest that they create stable messages?

vegetarians might construct a reading that considers how cows are exploited through farming, while dairy farmers or vets might produce an analytical assessment of the animal's physique or monetary worth.

In short, connotative readings are manufactured through our individual experiences and knowledge. This leads Hall to conclude that the individual signs that encode media products are multi-accentual and that media texts, as a whole, are polysemic (poly = many/semic = signs). In plain English, Hall is simply arguing that audiences read products in different ways, and that those differences are the result of their individual experiences. Some audience members might might form readings that are in line with the original intentions of product makers, while others will read against the grain of those intentions.

Media misreadings

Hall is careful to highlight the difference between misreading a media product and producing a reading that is knowingly oppositional. Misreading occurs, he suggests, when audiences do not have the capacity to fully understand a product's intended message. Misreadings can be formed as a result of the following:

- **Overly complex narratives.** Misunderstandings can be prompted when stories use overly complicated structures or where narratives are too experimental. Surrealist narratives or postmodern expositions might, if too difficult to follow, prevent an audience from decoding a product successfully.
- **Ideas are too alien.** Hall also suggests that misreadings can occur if the nature of content falls beyond the audience's everyday experience. For instance, a news story that narrates the attempted migration of refugees from a war-torn country might be so far

removed from the everyday experiences of readers that they are unable to fully comprehend the intended encoding effects the story is trying to convey.

- **Language elements cannot be decoded.** Products can be undecipherable if they have been encoded using a foreign language or if they deploy vocabulary that is too complex for the intended reader.

Box 17.2 Apply it: do any of the set texts you have studied invite misreadings?

- Do any of your set texts construct narratives that are overly complex? What elements or moments of the narrative are particularly problematic?
- Because of their lack of dialogue and short length, music videos are particularly problematic in terms of generating misreadings. Are your set text music videos likely to produce misreadings? If not, how do they compensate for their lack of diegetic sound?
- Do any of the set texts you have studied use language that is too complicated for their intended target audience? What elements or moments of the narrative are particularly problematic?
- Do any of the products you have studied produce deliberately ambiguous messages? Does this make them impossible to decode?

Exemplar: *Riptide* **(Eduqas).** Vance Joy's *Riptide* music video delivers a non-traditional narrative, replacing linear storytelling with a postmodern exposition that is open to what Hall would call audience misreading. Intertextual references are made to the 1970s cult film *The Wicker Man* to construct an ironic female victim stereotype, while later scenes allude to the voyeuristic eroticisation of femininity we see in Bond movies. Vance Joy's video deconstructs gender whilst also offering a critique of pop culture's portrayal of femininity. Yet that postmodern complexity creates, in Hall's terms, the potential for audiences to misread the video. Moreover, the lack of dialogue within music videos generally makes them much harder to decode than those media forms that use diegesis and scripted speech to help anchor meaning. *Riptide's* deliberate attempt to disconnect the song's lyrics from accompanying imagery presents a further frustration, and ultimately renders the video unintelligible for most casual viewers.

Further set text help is available for a range of products for all exam boards at www.essentialmediatheory.com

---

Concept 2: dominant, negotiated and oppositional decoding

Cultural hegemonies

Hall applies Antonio Gramsci's concept of hegemony to suggest that an invisible set of rules governs and directs our behaviours and beliefs. Hegemonies, Hall argues, define what we think is '"natural", "inevitable", "taken for granted" about the social order' (Hall, 1999, 516). More importantly, the mainstream media, he suggests, plays a crucial role in maintaining and reinforcing those dominant ideologies.

It could be argued, for instance, that newspapers endorse and reinforce the legitimacy of our parliamentary system through reportage. Political stories often feature as front page leads, helping to reinforce the authority of our political leaders. Deferential interviews might convince us that politicians work to affect our best interests. News media might also persuade us that a private school education or a professional background makes for the best political leaders and, as such, that it is natural that the upper middle classes dominate our political system.

These ideas, of course, are not 'natural' or 'common sense'. They are, in Hall's terms, social constructs, shared and distributed in a way that helps to maintain the power of those who dominate and control our social structures. Hall, moreover, argues that those who wield

---

Box 17.3 Think about it: what evidence is there to suggest that your set texts reinforce dominant ideologies?

- What messages do the set texts encode regarding social power? Who do they suggest ought to be in control? Who are our 'natural' leaders?
- What messages do the set texts encode regarding gender and power? What roles do those products suggest are natural for males and females?
- What messages do your set texts encode regarding race and power?
- Can we really conclude that the contemporary media industry solely reflects dominant ideologies? In what ways do your set texts encode subversive messages?

social power maintain authority *because* they control the media or are able, at the very least, to forge close relationships with media makers so that their vision of the world is communicated as 'natural' or 'inevitable'.

Of course, hegemonies and dominant ideologies are not static. The hegemonic ideas that come to dominate have to be applied and reapplied via the continuous stream of material that is authored by the media. The authors of that media, moreover, change continuously: audiences seek out new voices, while marginalised social groups find ways to make themselves heard within mainstream discourse. And, much like high street fashion or the ephemeral nature of a music trend, we find that hegemonic ideas become outworn and are discarded while a continuous stream of new ideas bubble to the surface as replacements.

Cultural resistance and hegemonic agreement

Media producers might encode messages that reinforce dominant ideologies, but it is not necessarily true that all audience members will submit to those ideas in a passive or submissive manner. On the contrary, Hall suggests that audiences engage in a continuous assessment of the media they consume and, as a result, they can resist any hegemonic encodings they might construct.

Audiences, Hall tells us, create readings using 'situated logics' (Hall, 1999, 516) – filtering the world according to their individual knowledge and experience. A benefits claimant, for example, who has experienced poverty and hardship as a result of a benefits sanction will be less likely to accept a media message that promotes austerity politics. A life-long Labour Party supporter might similarly decode the right-leaning *The Daily Mail* with a degree of scepticism while, conversely, the same 'situated logics' might lead Conservative Party voters to dismiss a *The Guardian* editorial as equally misleading.

Hall argues that the following groups of media decoding are possible if we take into account the potential effects of contextual factors and 'situated logics':

- **Dominant readings:** audiences decode media products and accept the dominant cultural messages produced by a product. Here, audiences knowingly agree with the hegemonic messages constructed by professional media.

- **Negotiated readings:** audiences might produce a negotiated reading if the encoder's message is acknowledged in general terms, but individual experiences lead an audience member to question or resist some aspects of the message. Thus, audiences knowingly agree with some of the hegemonic statements produced by professional media while questioning other aspects.

- **Oppositional readings:** audiences understand the message but refuse to believe it or use their personal experience/ideological viewpoint to challenge the message produced. In this way, audiences knowingly produce a contrary reading of the hegemonic statements produced by the media.

Box 17.4 Apply it: what multiple readings of your set texts can audiences produce?

Use these questions to help you identify how dominant, oppositional or negotiated readings of your set texts might be constructed by different audience groups:

- How might the political beliefs of the audience lead them to construct negotiated or oppositional decodings? What might these oppositional decodings be?
- How might the social class of readers lead them to produce an alternative reading of your set texts?
- How might males and females react differently to the set texts you are studying?
- In what ways might a contemporary audience react differently to the historical set texts you have studied? In what ways does their contemporary experience enable them to construct oppositional readings?

Exemplar: *The Daily Mail* front page, Thursday 14 December 2017 (OCR and AQA). Under the editorial stewardship of Paul Dacre, *The Daily Mail* clearly took an editorial stance that was designed to appeal to a right-wing readership. *The Daily Mail* championed the merits of a hard Brexit – the 'Proud of Yourselves' front page accused MPs who voted against the advancement of the EU exit of being traitors of democracy. The newspaper encodes the hegemonic championing of British democratic values, positioning the reader to view Brexit as a democratic necessity. A right-wing readership will, most likely, create a dominant reading – agreeing that the parliamentarians in question are 'malcontents'. Yet, a left-wing readership would inevitably decode the *The Daily Mail's* messages differently – using their contextual knowledge of the newspaper's bias and their own beliefs to construct a contrary view of the MPs.

Further exemplar paragraphs for set texts from all exam boards are available at www.essentialmediatheory.com

Table 17.1 Speak Stuart Hall

Decoding	Media audiences read the messages that producers construct.
Dominant readings	Dominant readings occur when audiences knowingly decode texts in the way they were intended by media makers. Audiences agree with any hegemonic encodings.
Encoding	Media institutions encode media products – using honed processes and strategies to produce media products that communicate messages to their audiences.
Hegemony	The set of ideas that dominate within society – these ideas are usually formed by those groups who have power. Hegemonies often legitimise the power of elite social groups. The media plays a key role in distributing hegemonic messages to all sections of society.
Misreading	An audience reading that fails to correctly decode the intended meaning of a media product as a result of its complexity or illegibility.
Negotiated readings	Negotiated readings occur when audiences both resist and accept the messages constructed by a media product.
Oppositional readings	Oppositional readings occur when audiences use their individual knowledge, beliefs or experiences to construct a contrary reading of a media text.
Situated logics	Refers to kinds of experience, knowledge and beliefs that an individual audience member has when decoding a product. This might also refer to the physical environment in which decoding occurs.

Table 17.2 Hall: ten minute revision

Concept 1: *Encoding and decoding*
- Professional media encodes messages using visual and aural cues.
- Media encoding is affected by institutional context, media production processes and genre-driven routines.
- Media products are polysemic as a result of their use of visual signs.
- Audiences do not necessarily decode the meanings that media producers effect in a straightforward way.
- Audiences can misread products if they are too complex or are untranslatable.

Concept 2: *Dominant, negotiated and oppositional readings*
- Media products reinforce dominant ideologies and cultural hegemonies.
- Dominant ideologies are subject to change – again, the media plays a crucial role in effecting those changes.
- Audiences use 'situated logics' to decode media messages.
- Audiences can produce readings of products that accept the dominant ideologies they construct.
- Audiences can use their contextual knowledge to read against the grain of a media product and to thus produce negotiated or oppositional decodings.

Three theorists who might challenge Hall's thinking
- **George Gerbner:** would suggest that audiences find it difficult to resist the effects of media products. Gerbner's mainstreaming theory would suggest that even the least susceptible audience members experience attitudinal change as a result of media exposure.
- **Albert Bandura:** his Bobo doll experiments would suggest that the media has a causal effect on audience behaviours and prompts audiences to copy behaviours they have seen in the media.
- **David Gauntlett:** would argue that media products do not necessarily reinforce cultural hegemonies. Contemporary media products offer a wide range of identities and subversions that often work in opposition to dominant ideologies.

18 Fandom

Henry Jenkins

Jenkins' research represents, in many senses, an extension of Stuart Hall's audience reception model in that fan readings of professional media, according to Jenkins, often produce oppositional responses to the meanings intended by their creators. Indeed, fandoms, for Jenkins, are visible markers of an audience's capacity to produce aberrant readings of professional media and provide, moreover, substantial evidence that audiences are active media consumers.

Jenkins' later academic research is similarly interested in the way that audiences consume the media, examining the impact that digital technologies have had on audience–producer relationships. Jenkins traces two major effects of the digital revolution: first, that media producers and their audiences have converged as a result of digital networking effects – that, in other words, viewers and creators have forged a closer relationship as a result of digital networking; and, second, that audiences are increasingly engaging in what he calls participatory culture. Participatory culture, in Jenkins' view, covers a wide range of DIY media practices, but it is principally affected when audiences use technologies to form online communities. For Jenkins, the exponential growth of participatory culture is a media game changer in that it empowers audiences to effect wider social change.

Concept 1: fan appropriation

In his groundbreaking 1992 book, *Textual Poachers*, Jenkins engages in what he calls an 'ethnographic' study of fandoms – an insider's account of how fans build communities. Jenkins was particularly interested in the print-based fanzines of the pre-internet era whose lo-fi products were distributed by old-fashioned mail and authored by amateur writers who were keen to share the stories they had written in response to shows such as *Blake 7, Doctor Who* and *Star Trek*.

Jenkins' analysis suggested that those early fan communities were far more complex than they first appeared or were given credit for. 'Fan culture,' he tells us, 'reflects both the audience's fascination with programs and [the] fans' frustration over the refusal/inability of producers to tell the kinds of stories viewers want to see' (Jenkins, 2013, 162).

Jenkins argues that fanfiction plugs the gap that exists between the needs of audiences and the commercially safe output of the shows they watch. Jenkins groups fanfiction output using the following categories:

- **Recontextualisations** are fan produced stories that fill in missing scenes or provide backstory to explain character actions from a particular moment in a product narrative.
- **Expanded series timelines** provide imagined sequels for a particular show. The short-lived 1980s cult hit *Blake 7*, for example, was a particular frustration for fans who wanted the BBC to recommission it. Fans invented their own sequels when it became clear that the BBC was not going to commission any new episodes.
- **Refocalisations** construct stories that reposition minor or secondary characters as central protagonists.
- **Moral realignments** supply antagonists and villains with backstories that explain their dark motives and morally dubious character traits.
- **Crossovers** are stories in which characters from one show might be placed within the context/timeline of another product. *Doctor Who's* TARDIS, for instance, might appear in the middle of a *Star Wars* sequence.
- **Personalisations** are stories that place the amateur author at the centre of a professional narrative. The writer might play a heroic role or develop a romantic engagement with a product's protagonist.
- **Eroticisation:** Jenkins suggests that 'fan writers, freed of the restraints of network censors, often want to explore the erotic dimensions of characters' lives' (Jenkins, 2013, 175). In the liberated world of fanfiction, eroticisation gives free reign to audiences who want to move beyond the secret nods and winks that are made within TV shows to create reworked (and subversive) adult reimaginings of character interaction.

Reconstructing hypermasculinity/realigning heteronormativity

Erotic fanfiction, perhaps, contributes most to the lay perception of fan activity as a marginal, slightly seedy exercise carried out by obsessive nerds; but it is this category of fan activity that attracted the most significant analysis by Jenkins. His early research focused on a sub-genre of slash fanfiction in which heterosexual lead characters are repositioned within gay storylines. Slash fiction might engineer, for instance, a sexual liaison between two lead males or create stories that resolve in a romantic union between a product's masculine hero and their erstwhile male nemesis.

Jenkins' asserts, importantly, that slash fiction is often written by heterosexual female audiences who are writing to express their frustration at the dominance of hypermasculine tropes within mainstream television. Female audiences, Jenkins suggests, yearn for male characters who are less aggressive, and, in their absence, they use fanfiction to reconstruct their on-screen heroes to represent a sensitive or more feminised ideal.

Jenkins, too, alerts us to the marginalisation of gay characters within mainstream television, suggesting that the widescale absence of lesbian, gay, bisexual and transgender (LGBT) representations is negotiated by fans through imaginative reworkings in their fanfiction. Jenkins also suggests that source texts often provide the starting points for these appropriations – a male character might nod in a suggestive manner to a secondary male; dialogue might offer a hint of forbidden love. The writers of slash fiction merely pursue the subtle cues laid down by a show's professional writers, who, Jenkins tells us, are restrained from producing overt gay storylines by the commercial imperative to keep stories 'straight'.

Box 18.1 Think about it: fanfiction and textual poaching

- Is today's media landscape dominated by a narrow range of character representations? Think about the stock characters used in TV drama in terms of gender, class, age or ethnicity.
- Examine the fanfiction that surrounds your TV set texts. In what ways does fan activity evidence the idea that audiences are active consumers?
- Does fan activity fill in any representation gaps present in the set text?

Concept 2: audience–producer convergence in the digital age

Fan communities

By sharing fanfiction with like-minded others, individual audience members can forge connections with a wider community. Importantly, Jenkins tells us, the development of the internet has facilitated an exponential explosion of textual poaching practices while also prompting a convergence of audience–producer relations. While fans were once reliant on the physical distribution of their fan output through print-based products, digital media, with its peer-to-peer networking capabilities, has sped up the process of fan communication and enabled a wider scope of fan networks.

The digital revolution has impacted on fandom in the following ways:

- **Digital technologies have given fans a new range of tools to express their voice.** While traditional fandoms relied heavily on fanzines, contemporary fan culture works within a wider scope of formats, including video remixes, YouTube parodies and recreations, mashups and fan-based artwork.
- **Digital networking has enabled an ever-widening diversity of professional media to have fan followings.** While fan communities were once restricted to products that had a cult status, fandoms are now attached to nearly all film and TV media. From *Songs of Praise* to *Star Wars*, from *My Little Pony* to *Lego*, most media products have a social media community connected to them.
- **Fan engagement can be realised in real time.** Through contemporary digital networks, fans share, interact and communicate with one another both during and immediately after broadcast transmissions.

Audience power, digital media and instant feedback

Fandom has also enabled what Jenkins calls 'consumer activism' (Jenkins, 2013, 175), whereby the instantaneous reactions of audience members adhere to form an informal focus group that speaks back to media producers. In this sense, fan engagement acts as a real-time assessment of a product's appeal. Media producers, moreover, are ever alert to the collective voice of these fan groups – soliciting and channelling fan interaction via Twitter hashtags to help shape the direction and content of their products.

Fans, however, can deliberately channel their collective voice into campaigns that are designed to change or boycott products. Online petitions and hashtag memes can be quickly orchestrated on social media to vent fan anger when a character is killed off or, potentially, to 'call out' more serious concerns regarding representation issues.

Nourishing fan bases to exploit the digital labour of audiences

Jenkins, too, outlines the extent to which contemporary media producers court and nourish fan bases to construct brand awareness and to maintain product loyalty. Audiences, he suggests, play an integral role in distributing and circulating modern media products through social media platforms. By inducing audiences to share or 'like' content online, media makers are able to market or advertise media for minimal cost.

In the traditional media landscape, fans and producers occupied distinctly separate territories. Fans consumed, while producers laboured in isolation to make the products that so occupied their audiences' interests. Both sides of this traditional consumption equation rarely interacted.

The digital media landscape, however, creates a much closer consumption relationship. Audiences and producers have converged, with audiences now playing an integral part in content development, while producers are ever more reliant on the digital labour of their audiences to market and distribute their products within the fragmented broadcast networks that make up the modern media landscape.

Social media tactics used to drive audience engagement

The following audience–producer convergence strategies are deployed by contemporary media products:

• **Transmedia storytelling.** Products are 'transmedia' if they are relayed across multiple platforms. Web-based content might outline character backstories. Twitter accounts might be used to give fictional characters a real-life presence. Transmedia storytelling

---

Box 18.2 Research it: diagnose the level of audience–producer convergence in your set texts

Use the following questions to help structure your research into the effects and scope of audience–producer convergence regarding your set texts.

Diagnosing audience effects on products

- In what ways do the media set texts you are studying construct audience feedback mechanisms? What Twitter hashtags do they use?
- What do the fans tell their producers on social media platforms?
- Have the set texts been subject to an online campaign to change any aspects?
- Has audience power shaped the set texts you are producing?

Diagnosing producer use of fan labour

- How do products take advantage of the digital labour of their fans to help market and distribute their products?
- Have trailers or other promotional material been released on YouTube? How many hits, reposts or 'likes' has this material gained?
- Do set text products deliberately nourish fan groups or fan activity? Do they make fan kits available for download? Have they constructed a fan wiki or an official fan website?

Further audience–producer convergence help sheets are available for set texts from all exam boards at www.essentialmediatheory.com.

---

rewards loyal fans with additional content while expanding the storytelling possibilities of the brand. Transmedia story formats, more importantly, give producers the ability to market their products through smartphone ownership and audience sharing.

- **Promotional preview material release.** Producers exploit fan power by releasing promotional material through fan networks. Using fan labour to market and advertise products is highly cost effective.
- **Twitter hashtags.** Fan debate can be successfully channelled using hashtags – this also allows producers to track fan opinion.

- **Product maker interactions.** Interviews, post-show web chats and 'behind the scenes' footage are incredibly easy ways to bring fans and producers together. These moments promote a personal engagement with products.
- **Fan repostings.** Audience engagement is further facilitated by reposting content or comments made by fans. In this way, media producers can construct a sense that they are engaging with fans at a personal level.
- **Textual poaching invites.** Products deliberately include material that is designed to prompt a fan response. For instance, when James Bond hints at his bisexual past in *Skyfall*, fans were invited to manufacture material that recontextualised 007's heterosexuality – directing Bond audiences to engage in textual poaching practices for the purpose of brand cultivation.
- **Competitions, giveaways and other loyalty rewards.** Products maintain the visibility of their brands by providing a steady stream of digital rewards. Giving away downloadable extras, fan kits, wallpapers and regular updates are all designed to keep products alive and their audiences primed for sequels or further releases.
- **Crossover events.** Products often team up with other brands to take part in joint events. Crossovers enable brands to gain exposure to other product's fan bases.

Box 18.3 Revise it: diagnose the use of social media to promote/distribute set texts

This activity is particularly useful for exam questions that ask you identify digital marketing strategies used by media producers. It can also be useful when discussing how set texts engage with their audiences through digital technology. Analyse relevant set texts using the following prompts:

- How has YouTube been used to market or advertise the product? Diagnose 'likes' or 'share' stats to help build a picture of the effectiveness of this strategy.
- In what ways do set texts used transmedia storytelling to enhance brand visibility?
- Research the social media tactics deployed by set text marketers. What notable strategies did they employ? How effective were they? What is innovative about their use of social media?

Exemplar 1: *Stranger Things* **(OCR) – use of fan power to market season two.** Most shows construct official fan pages and YouTube channels to distribute preview material and promos. The official Facebook fan page of the hit series *Stranger Things* has garnered over six million followers, while the release of the *Stranger Things* season two trailer received 330,000 'likes' on YouTube and prompted over 21,000 comments. It was no accident that the trailer was deliberately enigmatic, thus promoting a plethora of discussion and fan theorising before the first episode of the new season was aired. This marketing strategy deliberately took advantage of what Jenkins would call audience–producer convergence – exploiting fan labour to create an effective and cost free marketing plan for the product.

Exemplar 2: *Humans* **(Eduqas) – using transmedia storytelling to build brand engagement online.** The set text *Humans* was universally applauded for its transmedia storytelling marketing campaign. Before the series was initially aired on Channel 4, audiences were encouraged to visit a fake website that supposedly sold robots from the Synthetica Persona factory. Fans could arrange for the collection of defunct models, while an online discussion feature on the site allowed audiences to converse with imaginary customer service personnel. Another layer of authenticity was constructed with the creation of character-based Twitter accounts that fed live tweets regarding the show's narrative direction. Transmedia storytelling was thus designed to encourage fan power and create a cost-effective marketing campaign to engage audiences in advance of the episode one broadcast.

Further set text help is available for a range of products for all exam boards at www.essentialmediatheory.com

Concept 3: fans use participatory culture to effect wider social change

Cyber utopianism and Nicholas Negroponte

In many senses, Jenkins is a torch bearer for a largely optimistic view of the internet's potential. Nicholas Negroponte was one of the first commentators to recognise the earth-shattering potential of the web during its infancy in the 1990s. 'The information superhighway,' Negroponte wrote in 1995, 'may be mostly hype today, but it is an understatement about tomorrow. It will exist beyond people's wildest predictions' (Negroponte, 1995, 231). Negroponte, like Jenkins, embraced the digital revolution with open arms. Digital technology, he argued, will be 'a natural force drawing people into greater world harmony' (Negroponte, 1995, 230). 'We will socialise in digital neighbourhoods in which physical space will be irrelevant,' he prophesied, 'The digital planet will look and feel like the head of a pin' (Negroponte, 1995, 6).

Negroponte's optimism regarding digital technology can be grouped into the following arguments – these are equally applicable to Jenkins' view of contemporary digital media:

- **Personalisation:** the internet will enable us to consume media/information that is tailored to our needs and desires.
- **Democratisation:** because no one is in charge of the internet, it is immune from the abuses of large-scale organisations, governments or powerful multinational companies. The internet is a space in which every voice can be heard.
- **Miniaturisation:** the internet will make the world a smaller place. Ideas are globally shared, resulting in the collapse of cultural differences and the erosion of social divisions.

Jenkins – the cyber utopian

Jenkins' thinking mirrors much of Negroponte's early cyber optimism. 'Audiences,' Jenkins argues, 'empowered by these new technologies… are demanding the right to participate' (Jenkins, 2006a, 24). New technologies, he suggests, both democratise and miniaturise the world in that they provide ordinary audiences with the means to participate in wider social discussions. Participatory culture gives us all a voice, Jenkins argues, with communities forming around these digital discussions in ways that clearly mimic Negroponte's 'digital neighbourhoods'.

Jenkins is careful, however, to distinguish the practices that constitute participatory culture from the wider term 'Web 2.0'. For Jenkins, Web 2.0 defines a wide range of *commercial* activities that major media corporations use across the web – product distribution, sales/marketing functions and so forth. Stripped to its essential core, Web 2.0 is a business model driven by profit.

Participatory culture, Jenkins argues, is distinctly different in that its motives are community and knowledge oriented. Participatory culture exists not to make money, but to allow its members to exchange information, and to express themselves creatively while also providing a space in which fan creations can be shared with others.

From cultures to online participation

The roots of participatory culture, Jenkins claims, can be found in the folk traditions that preceded the mass media era – in the songs and music that working-class musicians shared with one another before mass radio broadcasting. Participatory culture today can be located in the amateur arts groups and drama clubs – places where ordinary people can create, share and experiment. And, Jenkins suggests, these communities have, in part, migrated to become digital networks – existing alongside, yet distinctly different to, the commercial activities of Web 2.0.

What excites Jenkins most about participatory culture is its value as an identity enabler. The online fanfictions written in response to traditional media products give voice to an audience's desires and needs. Peer-to-peer videos fill the gaps that professionally produced media products cannot or will not occupy. And, in making and sharing DIY media, fans are engaging in community-based discussion.

Jenkins, moreover, perceives that the internet has the capacity to translate that discussion into political engagement. We can see that process in action when we look at the #MeToo campaign that formed in response to the Harvey Weinstein allegations. What started out as a Hollywood scandal concerning the alleged abuse of women by media mogul Harvey Weinstein quickly mushroomed into an online global campaign, to protest against misogyny and male abuse more generally. Jenkins, too, draws our attention to the Harry Potter Alliance – an organisation that has channelled fan power into global political activism through its campaigns to promote worldwide gender equality, among other things.

Box 18.4 Discuss it: in what ways is the internet a force for social good?

- Is the internet a force for social good? What concrete evidence can you present to support arguments that it exerts a positive influence on society?
- Can you think of any online campaigns that have tried to create social change? Have they been effective?
- In what ways does the internet create purposeful communities?

The cult of the amateur

Jenkins, however, can be criticised for the one-sided nature of his discussion – for presenting, perhaps, an over-inflated optimism regarding the potential benefits of our digital networks. In his 2008 book, *The Cult of the Amateur*, Andrew Keen draws attention to the effect that user-generated content has had in terms of shifting the quality of our media experiences. Keen mourns the loss of traditional media production, arguing that professionally-produced content is made by highly trained media specialists who work, for the most part, with ethical integrity. For Keen, traditional media production is important because it fulfils a gatekeeping function. Traditional media filters our news so that only the most reliable information becomes public, and it further filters cultural production so that the best music, the best film and the best TV are visible.

Conversely, participatory culture allows amateur journalists to unwittingly mislead us or to radicalise our viewpoints with one-sided debate. Participatory culture might have democratised the media, but it has also allowed fake news to garner as much attention as authentic journalism. Participatory culture might have given us a remix culture, but even the most cursory look at YouTube will reveal an endless stream of second rate products – cat videos and vlogs made by product-sponsored influencers.

Jenkins neatly divides professional and amateur production in two, suggesting that audiences are able to disentangle these distinct strands. But, for Keen, the divide between those two worlds has blurred – and that is problematic. YouTube vlogging gives us authentic content, he

---

Box 18.5 Discuss it: in what ways is the internet problematic?

- How has social media affected political debate in the UK?
- Look carefully at the user comments on the online versions of your newspaper set texts – how would you describe the tone of the debate? Is the commentary problematic?
- Do people really use YouTube to create peer-to-peer connections or has it been hijacked for more commercial purposes?
- In what ways is the internet controlled by a handful of global companies? In what ways is their dominance problematic?

suggests, yet others work as nothing more than extended advertorials that are designed to subtly and unknowingly coerce us into buying sponsored content.

Keen, too, critiques the indexing system that controls our access to the internet, arguing that Google and YouTube search engine rankings are governed, for the most part, by popularity rather than any notion of accuracy. The sites that are visited the most are ranked the highest, whether or not the information they communicate is useful, skilfully researched or relevant. Thus, we have to temper Jenkins' notion that digitally-driven participatory culture is a force for good with the idea that the net is equally capable of misleading us.

Table 18.1 Speak Henry Jenkins

Audience–producer convergence	The coming together of media producers and audiences, principally through digital communications.
Cyber dystopianism	The belief that digital technologies have an adverse effect on society.
Cyber utopianism	The belief that digital media can and is creating positive social change.
Media democratisation	Placing media power in the hands of ordinary audience members.
Fan labour	The work, often free of charge, executed by fans and audiences to distribute or construct media for larger companies.
Participatory culture	The use of DIY media by audiences – usually to effect change or to share information. Participatory culture is not devised for commercial purposes.
Textual poaching	Appropriating media products for purposes that were not originally intended.
Transmedia storytelling	Using multiple media platforms to tell stories.
Web 2.0	The commercial activities of the web.

Table 18.2 Jenkins: ten minute revision

Concept 1: *fans appropriate media texts, producing readings that are not fully authorised by media producers*
- Jenkins suggests that audiences are able to use professional texts as 'creative scaffolding' on which they craft their own readings of products.
- Textual poaching can be used by marginalised fans to explore alternative readings to mainstream culture.
- Textual poaching in the digital age can take many forms, including fanfiction, remix culture, fan art or video parodies.

Concept 2: *fans and media makers have converged as a result of digital technology*
- Digital technologies have brought audiences and producers together.
- The digital revolution has expanded the scope of fandoms.
- Producers use their fans' digital labour to promote and market media.
- Contemporary media producers deliberately construct material to engage fan interest.

Concept 3: *fans use participatory culture to effect wider social change*
- Participatory culture is distinctly different from the commercial activities of Web 2.0.
- Participatory culture allows individuals to share and develop ideas with a like-minded community.
- Participatory culture can create social change.

Three theorists who might challenge Jenkins' thinking
- **James Curran and Jean Seaton:** argue that the internet is dominated by an oligopoly of commercial companies thus minimising the potential effects of participatory culture.
- **David Hesmondhalgh:** might agree that the internet has resulted in audience–producer convergence, but would argue that the media industry is still heavily reliant upon traditional marketing activities to reduce product risk. Media makers might engage in fan-based listening activities to construct or adapt products, but formulaic product design (using stars/ genre codes) remains a consistent focus of product content.
- **Sonia Livingstone and Peter Lunt:** suggest that the global nature of the net and the volume of material uploaded make effective regulation very difficult. New technology might open up the media to democratising forces and the development of new communities, but it is also open to potential abuse.

---

19 The end of audience

Clay Shirky

'We are living,' Shirky tells us, 'in the middle of the largest increase in expressive capability in the history of the human race' (Shirky, 2008, 106). The economic and social impact presented by the digital revolution, he suggests, can be compared to that of Gutenberg's printing press in the fifteenth century. Gutenberg's invention, perhaps, makes him the great-grandfather of mass communication, and by placing English translations of the Bible in the hands of ordinary citizens he assisted in the overthrow of religious and state power as it stood in the late medieval period. Shirky argues that the internet roll-out has had an equally revolutionary impact, placing mass communication tools in the hands of audiences, democratising media production so that ordinary people can organise and communicate widescale social change.

Concept 1: everybody makes the media

Communications and broadcast media technologies

The emergence of new communications technologies in the late nineteenth and early twentieth centuries – the telephone, fax machines, pagers and so forth – allowed mass one-to-one communications to take place over distances that had previously presented senders and receivers with enormous obstacles. The twentieth century also bore witness to the parallel development of a range of broadcast media technologies that kindled a one-to-many communications revolution.

Shirky argues, too, that the broadcast media of the twentieth century – cinema, radio and television – are a historical anomaly in that the dominance of these forms within our leisure time has created and nurtured audience passivity. Broadcast media consumption, Shirky claims, means that 'at work we're office drones, at home we're couch potatoes' (Shirky, 2010, 11). At no other point in history, he infers, were audiences as subdued as they were in the latter half of the twentieth century.

Shirky also points to the respective public and private characters of those newly emergent twentieth-century communications technologies. Telephone-based conversations, Shirky explains, take place between just two participants, while the contents of those one-to-one communications are typically private in nature. Conversely, broadcast media is designed for public consumption and the scale and expense of the equipment needed to make broadcast-quality content limits the production of television, film or radio products to a small number of well-placed organisations that have the necessary financial clout to make them. Television communication might create content that is publicly distributed, but the limited number of creators engaged in manufacturing content effects a one-to-many communications dynamic. And that, in Shirky's view, means that twentieth-century media power lay in the hands of the few rather than the many.

The digital revolution: the convergence of personal and broadcast media forms

Shirky argues that the advances made to computer-processing power during the early 1990s enabled communications and broadcast media technologies to converge. The miniaturisation of that technology enabled, in short, the invention of devices that could be used for both private and public communication. Email, for example, can be directed to a single recipient (one-to-one communication) or can be broadcast as a marketing mailshot (one-to-many communications). A similar blurring of broadcast and personal communication technologies is enabled through social media in that users can direct messages to single followers within their networks, or post updates to larger groups.

Digital innovation, Shirky further argues, substantially reduced the production barriers that prevented audiences from making their own broadcast media. YouTube users, for example, can make their own content and distribute it to mass audiences without the need to own prohibitively expensive production studios or editing suites. Likewise, Instagram and Twitter users can garner followings that rival the audience reach of established lifestyle magazines or traditional media broadcasters using nothing more than smartphone technology.

The simultaneous merging of public/private technologies, coupled with the reduction of broadcast entry barriers, leads Shirky to conclude that contemporary digital media exists as a spectrum of personal and broadcast media effects. At the communications end of that spectrum we find small-scale, close-knit groups who share content within the confines of a secure messaging group. Think here of an extended family unit using WhatsApp to share personal photographs or of a group of classmates using a messaging network to collaborate on a homework project. Social media of this kind shares the same hallmarks as the communications-based technologies of old: conversations are constructed for a private audience and are two-way in nature.

Digital media and mass amateurisation

Shirky also highlights the potential for contemporary audiences to use peer-to-peer digital networking to cultivate mass broadcast followings. Indeed, the power of the digital revolution is such that everyday users can procure the same kind of celebrity status that was once the sole preserve of cinema, television and radio. Shirky tells us that mass amateurisation in the contemporary age is effective because:

- **Amateur products can be distributed both quickly and on a global scale.** While traditional mass broadcasting relies on television and radio transmitters or on chains of cinemas, digital media can be globally distributed without any substantial financial outlay. Similarly, the production processes of traditional television broadcasters are incredibly slow when compared with the ability of YouTubers to make and distribute content at the touch of a button.
- **Digital distribution enables audience feedback.** The one-way communications dynamic of traditional mass broadcasting means that audiences are not able to provide feedback to producers. Digital media, conversely, reacts quickly to audience feedback, using 'likes', 'shares' and user-generated commentary to diagnose impact – often using that data to refine further content.

As a result, peer-to-peer digital networks now compete with, and in some instances have usurped, the reach of traditional mass broadcasting providers. But, Shirky suggests, any expansion of these amateur

---

Box 19.1 Think about it: the convergence of communications and broadcast media

- In what ways do your online set texts engage a 'communications'-oriented relationship with their audience?
- Do any of your online set texts exemplify mass amateurisation media?
- In what ways do these online mass amateurisation set texts exemplify Shirky's idea that online media quickly adopts a broadcast relationship when mass audiences are achieved?

---

networks comes at a cost. The larger one's audience, he argues, the more difficult it is to engage in meaningful conversations with any single recipient. What might begin as a one-to-one communication-oriented conversation turns into the impersonal one-way dynamic of a broadcast media relationship once a mass viewership is engaged.

The unusually short lifespans of some celebrity vloggers can perhaps be explained as a consequence of this dynamic, in that YouTubers often construct initial audience appeal through a personalised engagement with a small fan base. That initial intimacy, and potentially the authenticity of the vlog, becomes much harder to sustain as those fan bases expand.

Filter first, publish later

To ensure that the huge sums of money needed to make and distribute products are well spent, traditional media broadcasting, Shirky tells us, effects a robust filtering process. Quality controlling the content of traditional broadcast media, he explains, helps producers cultivate the mass audiences needed to justify or sustain production. The pre-vetting of content by traditional broadcasters is a necessity, Shirky argues, and ensures the valuable financial reserves of broadcasters are only spent on products that have the most potential to be popular and profitable. As a result, established editorial processes dominate traditional production. Quality control processes, Shirky further argues, can be readily applied to mass media because of the relatively small number of products that are made.

In the digital world, however, Shirky suggests that a 'publish first, filter later' mentality dominates. The ease with which digital media can be assimilated and published significantly reduces publication barriers, while the lack of traditional commercial overheads – salary expenses, taxation or more general running costs – means that amateur producers can publish higher risk content because the potential impact of failure is financially low. Indeed, Shirky claims that failure is an endemic feature of the internet and that the web is a space that invites constant experimentation: 'by reducing the cost of failure,' he writes, the web, 'enable[s] … participants to fail like crazy' (Shirky, 2008, 246).

The impossibility of pre-filtering

The 'publish first, filter later' model of the internet might invite experimentation, but the lack of editorial control enacted by digital content makers also presents some significant problems. Traditional broadcasters might be inclined to play it safe, but the editorial processes they use to control production perform a vital gatekeeping role. Those controls protect audiences from fake news or politically extreme content. They shield vulnerable audiences from excessively graphic material or explicit narratives. 'Mass amateurization,' Shirky thus argues, 'has created a filtering problem vastly larger than we had with traditional media, so much larger, in fact, that many of the old solutions are simply broken' (Shirky, 2008, 246). Indeed, the sheer volume of media uploaded to the internet today makes it almost impossible to check or corroborate content before it is published.

The future is digital

Traditional mass media might construct quality products with reliable and accurate content, but, Shirky concludes, their long-term chances of survival in today's digital world are slim. Digital networks and mass amateurisation, he argues, will inevitably come to dominate the media landscape. Shirky cites the following fatal flaws in the structure and scope of traditional mass media activity:

- The **high overhead costs of traditional media** (salaries, costs of premises, taxation) make them uncompetitive. In comparison, mass amateurisation oriented content can be made with much smaller budgets.
- The **slow decision-making processes** used to manage traditional media institutions make it harder for them to adapt to changing market conditions.

- Traditional media companies are **risk averse** as a result of the editorial processes used to ensure that programming achieves quality. Mass amateurisation oriented media operate a 'publish first, filter later' model that does not readily identify risk as a significant barrier.

Box 19.2 Discuss it: is Shirky right to suggest that traditional media is outmoded?

- Is Shirky right to suggest that the web has brought about a mass amateurisation revolution? Why do you agree or disagree?
- How has the loss of professional media gatekeeping disadvantaged audiences?

Consumers speak back to media makers

Digital innovation and mass amateurisation have placed significant pressures on traditional media makers, forcing them to radically rethink their production and distribution models or face extinction. And, in the same way that their audiences have used digital technology to mimic broadcasting, traditional broadcasters have reciprocated by integrating one-to-one communication within their production practices.

Newspapers now invite readers to comment on stories using online feedback tools. Video games connect and encourage player communication via online multiplayer features, while television makers encourage viewer conversations by deploying social media hashtags. Indeed, Shirky argues, those traditional media makers who resolutely fail to realise the importance of effecting a two-way conversation with their audiences will not survive the digital revolution. Contemporary consumers, he tells us, have come to expect that they can make contributions to the public conversations engaged by the broadcast media, and if mass broadcasters do not facilitate that need they will find that their services are no longer relevant. (See Table 19.1 for further details regarding the specific effects of the digital revolution in key areas of the media industry.)

Table 19.1 Effects of the digital revolution in key industries

Newspapers	• The explosion in blogs, online celebrity gossip, news sites and social media has contributed to declining readerships for newspapers. • The 'filter first, publish later' model adopted by newspapers means that their products often look and feel very safe when compared to their online competitors. Some newspapers have tried to combat this perceived safeness by recruiting provocative contributors (dubbed 'contrarians'). The *Daily Telegraph's* use of Boris Johnson as a column writer serves as an interesting example of this process. • Online newspapers have embraced the use of reader commentary to promote audience engagement. • Newspapers now operate a 'digital first' policy – breaking stories online as soon as they appear.
Television	• Television broadcasters have fought back, using YouTube as a marketing tool and also as a means to cultivate fan engagement through additional footage (behind the scenes clips, artist interviews, alternative edits). • Television and cable networks now sign successful YouTubers to make mass media content – capturing online experimental content that has found success. • Producers engage in web chats and other forums to effect personal connections with their audiences. • Television makers use Twitter hashtags to facilitate audience feedback or to promote audience conversations during broadcasts. Producers refer to this as 'second screening'. • Mainstream television's embrace of high-quality, multi-season, long-form storytelling offers products that YouTube cannot copy. This has helped traditional broadcasters maintain audience share.
Film marketing	• Services such as YouTube have helped level the playing field for independent film-makers giving them access to lucrative marketing and distribution channels. • Major production companies use YouTube analytics to help them predict the potential viability of a film release. Film companies determine where they ought to book cinemas and for how long using data gathered from marketing released on social media. • Much like television, producers use YouTube to garner publicity and interest through the release of additional material. • Persona marketing on social media platforms is used to mimic one-to-one connectivity between film-makers and their audiences. Fictional characters are often given a web presence to cultivate fan power.

Box 19.3 Apply it: diagnose the effects of the digital revolution on your set texts

- In what ways do your set texts deliver the benefits of digital technology?
- In what ways do your online set texts evidence a more experimental approach to content than their traditional media rivals?
- In what ways do your online set texts effect a more traditional one-to-many audience/producer broadcast relationship?
- In what ways have your broadcast media set texts been adversely affected by the digital revolution? Think here in terms of increased competition, diminishing advertising revenues or the potential reduction in quality that has occurred as a result of a general weakening of gatekeeping across all media sectors.
- In what ways have broadcast media set texts adapted to the digital revolution? How do they engage two-way conversations with their audiences?

Exemplar paragraphs that apply Shirky's ideas to set texts from all exam boards are available at www.essentialmediatheory.com

---

Concept 2: everyday communities of practice

Shirky argues that groups with shared interests, values or identities have always wanted to make contact with one another. In the pre-digital world, however, both physical and financial barriers prevented those groups from forming. In contrast, Shirky tells us, the internet roll-out has enabled the widespread construction of what he calls 'communities of practice'. The internet, he argues, enables groups of individuals to overcome the physical barriers of the pre-digital world, and 'the groups, once assembled, can be quite robust in the face of indifference or even direct opposition from larger society' (Shirky, 2008, 210).

Communities of practice are notable, Shirky suggests, for the following reasons:

- They are capable of creating social change. The flash mobs that propelled the Arab Spring, for instance, were enabled by social media activism that helped topple a series of repressive regimes.

**Box 19.4 Think about it: communities of practice –
good or bad?**

- What examples of online activism have you encountered that have
prompted positive social change or allowed marginalised groups to
have a more powerful voice?
- What recent examples of negative online behaviour can you
identify that have had adverse real world consequences?

- They are incredibly resilient when threatened – online communities
can disband and regroup very easily when threatened or censored.
- They are self-policing and driven by non-profit motives.
- They can also coalesce around socially undesirable subjects. Shirky
highlights, for example, the challenge that pro-anorexia groups
have presented in promoting dangerous lifestyle choices to vulnerable young women. Online political or religious extremism, too,
fans real-world violence.

The 'bargain' of audience engagement

Shirky also suggests that audiences and producers are engaged in a
transactional exchange when media products are consumed and that
audience–producer relationships are defined through an unofficial
'bargain' that is brokered between both parties. In traditional media
consumption, that transactional bargain is relatively straightforward in
that hard cash is usually exchanged to view a product. Money is traded
for a cinema ticket or a cable television subscription: media purchases,
in other words, produce the promise of a viewing pleasure.

The bargains made online, however, are complicated by the fact
that we expect to receive content, for the most part, without spending
any real money. This does not mean that online consumption is trans-
action free. On the contrary, vlogging viewers can only consume the
uploads posted if they watch the commercial advertising that precedes
them. The bargain made by audiences when reading online news is
that you allow internet cookies to be installed so that personalised
advertising can be displayed alongside story content.

Shirky's 'bargain', interestingly, also governs the kinds of conduct
that audiences unofficially agree among themselves as acceptable for

the online communities in which they participate. The rules governing online comment etiquette are not necessarily written down – they exist as an unofficial agreement that has been negotiated by users about the way they ought to behave when conversing with one another online. In online fandoms, for instance, it is universally accepted that stories are not shared for commercial gain or that you do not steal a fellow author's work.

The most interesting feature of the bargain, for Shirky at least, is that digital audiences can exercise a form of collective power that can shape or even determine the rules that govern their media engagement. If, collectively, we all decide that YouTube advertising is so obtrusive that we stop watching it, then the service would have no choice but to revise its commercial strategy. In short, audiences have the power to shape online media content and, furthermore, have the communication tools to effect collective action against services if the need arises.

Shirky argues, too, that while the rules that govern small-scale communities of practice are easily and clearly defined, those same bargains

---

Box 19.5 Apply it: big services do not always produce beautiful effects

- Identify the 'bargain' that allows audiences to use your online set texts for free. What do users unofficially agree to in order to access free content?
- In what ways do producers create benefits for themselves as a result of making online content free?
- In what ways does internet advertising compromise the experience of online browsing?
- In what ways does online advertising compromise the integrity of set text content?

Challenge question

- In what ways do the large-scale audiences of your set texts inevitably lead to audience conflict? How, for instance, do reader comments on online news sites demonstrate a clash of expectations?

Exemplar paragraphs that apply Shirky's ideas to set texts from all exam boards are available at www.essentialmediatheory.com

tend to break down when products achieve mass audiences. An online fan group with less than 100 members will communicate within a clear set of expectations that are shared by all members. Posts that infringe those rules will be speedily censored or removed. Those rules breakdown, however, when online communities become larger and produce competing subgroups that will inevitably shape their own rules of engagement.

Thus, the large-scale nature of digital giants like Facebook or Twitter will inevitably lead, in Shirky's view, to a conflict of user interests. Such platforms promise interconnectivity and provide the necessary tools to enable those promises, but the scope and scale of the subgroups that operate within their networks will inevitably employ the site for purposes that are contradictory.

Table 19.2 Speak Clay Shirky

Broadcast media	Broadcast media (television, radio, newspapers) act like a megaphone enabling one-to-many communications. Information, in a broadcast relationship, will usually flow in one direction, from the sender to the receiver.
Communications media	Communications media (telephones and faxes) effect a two-way relationship in which senders and receivers are engaged in private conversations.
Digital communications convergence	Digital technologies have merged broadcast and communications media effects. Emails, for instance, can be both private and public – they can also have single or multiple recipients.
Gatekeeping	Limiting access to information – usually affected by traditional media broadcasters to maintain the quality of their products.
Mass amateurisation	The use of digital media by everyday audiences to produce broadcast media.
Second screening	Viewing traditional media while also engaging with accompanying content on another device. For example, using a mobile phone to join in a Twitter conversation while watching a television show.

Table 19.3 Shirky: ten minute revision

Concept 1: *everybody makes the media*
• Shirky highlights the revolutionary impact of digital technology in speeding up media production processes.
• Media consumption patterns have changed from a broadcast model that involves one sender and many recipients to a many-to-many model.
• Traditional media, Shirky argues, uses a 'filter then publish' model to provide quality content.
• Shirky suggests that the internet has resulted in a 'publish now, filter later' model due to lower production costs and reduced entry barriers to media production.

Concept 2: *everyday communities of practice*
• Audiences actively shape their own rules of engagement with professional media products.
• Digital technologies have resulted in an explosion of what Shirky calls 'communities of practice'.

Two theorists who might challenge Shirky's thinking
• **James Curran and Jean Seaton:** argue that the internet continues to be dominated by an oligopoly of commercial companies.
• **David Hesmondhalgh:** might agree that the internet has resulted in audience–producer convergence, but would argue that the media industry is still heavily reliant upon traditional marketing activities to reduce product risk.

Works cited

Bandura, A. (1973). *Aggression: A Social Learning Analysis*. Englewood Cliffs, NJ: Prentice-Hall.

Barthes, R. (2006). *S/Z*. Malden, MA: Blackwell.

Barthes, R. (2007). *Image, Music, Text*. New York: Hill and Wang.

Barthes, R. (2009). *Mythologies*. London: Vintage books.

Baudrillard, J. (1987). *The Ecstasy of Communication*. New York: Semiotext(e).

Baudrillard, J. (1995). *The Gulf War Did Not Take Place*. Bloomington, IN: Indiana University Press.

Baudrillard, J. (2018). *Simulacra and Simulation*. Ann Arbor, MI: University of Michigan Press.

BFI (2018). *Statistical Yearbook 2018* [online]. Available at: www.bfi.org.uk/sites/bfi.org.uk/files/downloads/bfi-statistical-yearbook-2018.pdf [Accessed 9 April 2019].

Bignell, J. (2002). *Media Semiotics*. Manchester: Manchester University Press.

Black Lives Matter (2019). 'What We Believe' [online]. Available at: https://blacklivesmatter.com/about/what-we-believe/ [Accessed 15 April 2019].

Bush, G.W. (2002). 'State of the Union Address', 29 January, The Senate, Washington. Available at: www.washingtonpost.com/wp-srv/onpolitics/transcripts/sou012902.htm [Accessed 10 June 2019].

Butler, J. (2007). *Gender Trouble*. New York: Routledge.

Curran, J. and Seaton, J. (2010). *Power without Responsibility: Press, Broadcasting and the Internet in Britain*. 7th edn. London: Routledge.

Evans, J. and Hesmondhalgh, D. (2005). *Understanding Media: Inside Celebrity*. Maidenhead, UK: Open University Press.

Fuchs, C. (2014). *Social Media: A Critical Introduction*. London: Sage Publications.

Gauntlett, D. (2008). *Media, Gender and Identity*. London: Routledge.

Gauntlett, D. (2011). *Making Is Connecting*. Cambridge: Polity Press.

Gerbner, G. and Morgan, M. (2016). *Against the Mainstream*. New York: Peter Lang.

Giddens, A. (1991). *Modernity and Self-Identity*. Cambridge: Polity Press.

Gilroy, P. (2004). *After Empire*. Abingdon, UK: Routledge.

Gilroy, P. (2008). *There Ain't No Black in the Union Jack*. London: Routledge.

GLAAD (2019). 'Where We Are on TV' [online]. Available at: http://glaad.org/files/WWAT/WWAT_GLAAD_2018-2019.pdf [Accessed 12 April 2019].

Hall, S. (1999). 'Encoding/Decoding'. In: S. During, ed., *The Cultural Studies Reader*. 2nd edn. New York: Routledge.

Hall, S., Evans, J. and Nixon, S. (2013). *Representation*. 2nd edn. London: Sage Publications.

Hesmondhalgh, D. (2015). *The Cultural Industries*. 3rd edn. London: Sage publications.

hooks, b. (1982). *Ain't I a Woman*. London: Pluto Press.

Jenkins, H. (2006a). *Convergence Culture*. New York: New York University Press.

Jenkins, H. (2006b). *Fans, Bloggers and Gamers*. New York: New York University Press.

Jenkins, H. (2013). *Textual Poachers*. New York: Routledge.

Jenkins, H. (2019). 'Video Games Myths Revisited: New Pew Study Tells Us about Games and Youth' [online]. Available at: http://henryjenkins.org/blog/2008/10/video_games_myths_revisited_ne.html [Accessed 8 April 2019].

Keen, A. (2008). *The Cult of the Amateur*. London: Nicholas Brealey.

Keen, A. (2012). *Digital Vertigo*. New York: Constable & Robinson.

Lévi-Strauss, C. (2004). *The Savage Mind*. Oxford: Oxford University Press.

Lievrouw, L. and Livingstone, S. (2009). *Handbook of New Media*. London: Sage.

Livingstone, S. and Lunt, P. (2012). *Media Regulation*. London: Sage.

Merrin, W. (2005). *Baudrillard and the Media*. Cambridge: Polity.

Neale, S. (2001). *Genre and Hollywood*. London: Routledge.

Negroponte, N. (1995). *Being Digital*. New York: Vintage Books.

Procter, J. (2004). *Stuart Hall*. London: Routledge.

Propp, V. (2009). *Morphology of the Folktale*. Austin, TX: University of Texas Press.

Romero, M. (2018). *Introducing Intersectionality*. Cambridge: Polity.

Shirky, C. (2008). *Here Comes Everybody*. London: Allen Lane.

Shirky, C. (2010). *Cognitive Surplus*. London: Allen Lane.

Sweney, M. (2018). 'Out of Print: NME's Demise Shows Pressure on Consumer Magazines' [online]. *The Guardian*, 12 March. Available at: www.theguardian.com/media/2018/mar/12/nme-vogue-death-print-magazines [Accessed 8 April 2019].

Todorov, T. (1977). *The Poetics of Prose*. Oxford: Blackwell.

Townsend, M. (2019). 'Rise in UK Use of Far-Right Online Forums as Anti-Muslim Hate Increases' [online]. *The Guardian*, 16 March. Available at:

theguardian.com/world/2019/mar/16/rise-far-right-online-forums-anti-muslim-hate-wave [Accessed 7 April 2019].

UCLA (2018). 'Hollywood Diversity Report' [online]. Available at: https://socialsciences.ucla.edu/wp-content/uploads/2018/02/UCLA-Hollywood-Diversity-Report-2018-2-27-18.pdf [Accessed 15 April 2019].

van Zoonen, L. (1994). *Feminist Media Studies*. London: Sage.

Williams, P. (2013). *Paul Gilroy*. London: Routledge.

Index

Page numbers in **bold** denote tables.